ENTREPRENEURSHIP
EMPOWERED

ENTREPRENEURSHIP EMPOWERED

A New Millennium Business Guide
from Start Up to Succession

Companion Workbook

NATASHA M PALUMBO

Eternal Enterprise Publishing

First Printing: 2019

Second Edition Printing: 2020

ISBN: 978-1-7344905-0-3

Author Bio Photograph By: Juan Padilla with Luxus Photos

Book Cover Designed By: Joanne Jenkins and Natasha Palumbo with Ldy Bug Images

Edited By: Lauren Michelle

Eternal Enterprise Publishing

Sacramento, CA Ordering Information:

Special discounts are available on quantity purchases by corporations, associations, educators, and others. For details, contact the publisher at the above listed address.

U.S. trade bookstores and wholesalers:

Please contact Natasha M Palumbo

Tel: (916) 470-3330 or email natasha@entrepreneurshipempowered.com

Dedication

To my beautiful children, Allan and Annabella, I will love you for all time and eternity. You are my very reasons for living the EMPOWERED life. I encourage you to remember that love is the only thing that is real. Everything else is an illusion. Remember to always operate out of love, starting with yourselves, and be EMPOWERED!
You are both amazing!
You are Palumbos!

Contents

Acknowledgments

Father God, I thank You for the beautiful gift of life, Your eternal love, and amazing grace. Without You, I am nothing. But through You, I am Natasha M Palumbo, the daughter of the Most High. All honor and glory to Your name.

To my parents, I am eternally grateful. You all gave me several different gifts. Many of which you will see displayed in this book. Mom, thank you for the gift of creativity and a poetic use of words. Daddy and Bonnie, thank you for the gift of entrepreneurship. Remember there is no shame in speaking our truth, the good, the bad, and the ugly. In doing so we release ourselves from the bondage, take the keys back to our life, and become *Empowered!* I love you all.

To my best friend, Joanne Jenkins, thank you for being the one true person outside of my children that I trust with all of me. Thank you for all the support, not only for the time you have given to me during the writing of my book, but for all the constant support in my life. I am grateful for you. You are not only my best friend, you are my sister.

To my students, who inspired me to write *Entrepreneurship Empowered*, you are all very special to me. Professor P loves each of you and encourages you to live your life to the fullest. Dream and Do.

To my dear friend and mentor, Ron Hickey, thank you for guiding me through the writing process. For helping rewire my brain. For all the wisdom you bestowed upon me at each of our encounters. You are ridiculously amazing!

To my earthly angel who will remain unnamed, you completely saved me and blessed me a thousand-fold. I am eternally grateful, and I pray you receive a thousand back for all you have done for me. Thank you is simply not enough, but for now it will have to do.

Preface

To the reader, I want to thank you for your support. The fact that you are reading this book tells me that you are ready to be an Empowered Entrepreneur. You will find a wealth of information in this book. *Entrepreneurship Empowered* is full of up-to-date tools, strategies, and resources that will help you in life and business.

I am in the business of building up people who build businesses. I am honored to be able to help you build, too. You may visit my website at the address listed below. There you will find all the services and products I offer. I am a business adjunct professor with several colleges in the state of California, as well as a coach and consultant. I have been an entrepreneur since 2002. I am passionate about business and education. In addition to teaching, I host several workshops in the U.S., and I have a virtual *Entrepreneurship Empowered* online program. I firmly believe that we can and should live an *EMPOWERED* life. I would love for you to connect with me. You can find me on both LinkedIn and Instagram @ Natasha M Palumbo.

Be well,
Natasha M Palumbo, MBA

Author, Coach, Consultant, and Speaker
Entrepreneur – Educator – Empowered

www.entrepreneurshipempowered.com

Introduction: *Entrepreneurship Empowered*

Welcome to *Entrepreneurship Empowered: Companion Workbook*. This workbook is designed to guide you through the developing process of practical business planning. It is not, however, your traditional business planning guide. It is a new millennium, and business is done much differently in this era. First and foremost, you must be Empowered. You must understand yourself at a true and honest level. You must be able to embrace your God-given talents and authentic self. This workbook, along with *Entrepreneurship Empowered: A New Millennium Business Guide from Start Up to Succession*, will provide you with valuable resources, tools, hands-on activities, and personal growth activities in pursuit of helping you become EMPOWERED!

You will see that this companion workbook follows *Entrepreneurship Empowered*. However, this workbook has more activities than the actual book does. Many of the activities are designed to stretch you, which is required for growth. So, get ready to be stretched and get ready to grow. I want you to understand the importance of writing. Putting pen to paper stimulates a part of the brain called the Reticular Activating System (RAS). The RAS acts as a filter for everything your brain needs to process, giving more importance to the stuff that you're actively focusing on in that moment. The act of writing, which engages your motor skills, also helps keep the mind sharp. Therefore, this companion workbook is going to be so powerful because I am activating your mind in such a way that your RAS is firing off and your brilliance is about to pour out of you and flow into this workbook. I do want you to remember, however, that all the planning in the world is useless if there is no action behind it. You must always put the plan in action.

"In preparing for battle I have always found that plans are useless, but planning is indispensable."

—Dwight D. Eisenhower

The first activity you will find is a time management activity. This companion workbook is equipped with a planner. You will need to make sure you learn how to manage your time. If you are unable to manage your time, you will never be able to manage a business. You are encouraged to use the planner provided to block your time, schedule time you will work on projects, schedule time you will be working your normal work schedule, and I also encourage you to schedule your private time. You will also need to learn how to chunk your time. Chunking means to group similar activities together at the same time. For example, you pay bills all on the same day during a set time. You are going to need to learn to delegate and trust that the work you have delegated is going to get done. All too often, we are afraid to delegate because we have one of two issues: a control issue or a trust issue. You cannot build a business without trust and having complete control. You will never be able to grow without trusting your staff to do the jobs they were hired for. So, learn to delegate.

You must not procrastinate. Multitasking leads to procrastination. You believe you are doing so many things all at once, but what you are really doing is half a job here, half a job there, a quarter of a job over there, and so on. Our minds are not equipped to do multiple tasks at one time. Yes, you can start the laundry and then move to another task, but a machine is helping you do a task. You are not doing multiple tasks at one time when you are washing clothes or washing dishes if a machine is doing the work for you. Studies have shown that when you multitask, there is a 40% loss in productivity.[1] However, when you single task, you get your task done in a short amount of time. Those five tasks get done in two hours when you do one task at a time. When you multitask, it will take you five hours to get the same work done. Multitasking trains your brain to procrastinate. It's subtle, but the subconscious eats it right up.

One step in learning how to stop multitasking is to understand you have the right to your "no." Yes, you have the right to say no and to hear no. Many times, people are taking on more than what they can handle because they are not saying NO. Are you like that? Are you a people-pleaser? I sure was, then I realized a very valuable and powerful principle, which is now one of my top 10 Core Palumbo Principles: you have the right to your NO, and your YES is undeniable. This principle will be with me for my life, and I am not only using it for myself, but I am also sharing it with the world. Everyone needs to understand that no matter what, the dice of life will throw you a "no" time and time again. It is like a prison sentence. Until you take your power back, pick up those dice, shake them up in your hands, spit on them if you must, and throw them back to the world and, with everything you have inside yourself, you say, "MY YES IS UNDENIABLE!"

You must fully understand your relationship with time. Each of us has a different relationship with time. You may be surprised to find out that your relationship with time is tied to your trauma. I am a trauma expert—not by any fancy education, oh no. I am a trauma expert by the impact it has had on my life. I endured decades upon decades of abuse. I have endured more than most humans ever will. Yet, I stand before thousands of people and inspire them. Why? Because I have done almost a decade of therapy and will do decades more if needed. Therapy doesn't make me any less of a person. In fact, it increases my power. The more I get myself together, the greater the impact I get to make. Talk therapy is a start, but it will never do the trick on its own. Trauma is trapped inside the body. Our bodies have memory of good and bad. The trauma we endured as children often bleeds into adulthood. The therapy I am a big promoter of is EMDR. You can do a search for EMDR therapy and, in my book, *Entrepreneurship Empowered*, I tell you more about that type of therapy. Once you can get a handle on your therapy, the better off you will become. Understanding how time plays with your trauma and how you deal with it is very enlightening. If you are in one of my classes or my virtual Empowered Education series, you will be given a small reading. It regards your relationship with time. It is an excerpt from the book *Don't Let Anything Dull Your Sparkle* by Doreen Virtue. I highly recommend the book if you suffer from trauma. Everyone has trauma, either primary, secondary, or both. No one gets out without experiencing some type of trauma. Please know that you are not alone.

Before we move into the planner portion of this companion workbook, I would like to give you your first challenge. I try to do a challenge once a month when it comes to my health and wellness. I believe challenges are essential to helping us grow. They also keep me accountable as I post them on my social media and get others to join me. So, for your first Entrepreneurship Empowered Challenge, you are going to track your time. What do I mean? I mean just that. Track your time. You are going to have space provided where you can write down exactly everything you do with your time. So, from the moment you wake up till the moment you go to sleep, I want you to track your time. Write down what the time is and what you did during that time. In business, the more we track, the better we become. Tracking gives us valuable data. Data we can use to adjust, continue to do what works best, and stop doing what is wasteful and not working at all. In the long run, tracking saves us time and money. Many times, we are just wasting our time away. You will be surprised how much time you are wasting that could be redirected for better use. I will provide an example and room to track in the Challenge One section, which will be at the end of this introduction and right before the planner. Then, while you are tracking, I want you to move into blocking and scheduling your time. Use a pencil always when scheduling in a planner. That way when plans change, you can easily erase.

"Strategy is the art of making use of time and space. I am less concerned about the latter than the former. Space we can recover, lost time never."

—Napoleon Speaks

I would now like to explain how the companion workbook is constructed. You will see that it correlates with my book, *Entrepreneurship Empowered*. Chapter One, The Mind of an Empowered Entrepreneur, is all about exploring the way we think and self-awareness. The following activities will be found in Chapter One:
- Fixed/Growth Mindset
- What Does Your Mind Say About You?
- Self-Awareness
- Grit Test
- Creating Your "Why" Statement (also known as your Impact Statement)
- Goal Setting
- Creating a Vision Board

Chapter Two is Communication and Technology. Our world is rapidly changing, and both communication and technology are evolving alongside it. Because of technology, we communicate much differently than we ever have before. You must be digitally fluent, and you must master the art of communication in order to be an Empowered Entrepreneur. Both are mandatory. The following activities will be found in Chapter Two:
- Effective Communication
- Technology and Communication: How They Work Together
- Becoming More Digitally Fluent
- Microsoft Suite Challenge

Chapter Three, Types of Empowered Entrepreneurs, Business Legal Structure, and Intellectual Property, is one of the most complex chapters. There is no one set way to structure your business. You must do what is best for you and the type of Empowered Entrepreneur you plan to be. The following activities will be found in Chapter Three:

- Deciding What Type of Empowered Entrepreneur You Are
- Business Legal Structure
- Intellectual Property Search

Chapter Four is Business Planning. This chapter is where we really dive into the business plan, business canvas model, and pitch deck. You will start your pre-planning process in this chapter and do some preliminary brainstorming. The following activities will be found in Chapter Four:

- Business Planning
- Business Model Canvas Brainstorming Activity
- Pitch Deck Search
- Interviewing a Small Business Owner

Chapter Five is Marketing and Branding. This chapter has a lot of activities, and here you will be moving into the creation of your business. This part of the planning is very important, so do take time to really digest all that you are doing and being asked to do. Dig deeply. Do not be a surface dweller. You must go deep into thought and remove all elements of self-censorship. That way, what you are destined to create will be allowed to come forward with no hindrance. The following activities will be found in Chapter Five:

- Self-Branding Exercise
- Emotional Intelligence and Color Psychology Activity
- Name Creation
- Vision, Mission, and Value Development and SMARTER Business Goal Setting
- Slogan and Hashtag Development
- Market Research and Marketing Plan Development

"Marketing is no longer about the stuff that you make, but about the stories you tell."

—Seth Godin, author and entrepreneur

Chapter Six is Financial Planning, Accounting, and Funding Your Business. You must have an understanding of your money at all times. It is perfectly normal to hire people smarter than you, and I, for one, strongly encourage it. However, you must know what is going on with your accounts, and your financial well-being needs to be at the forefront of your thinking. The wealthy have a way of thinking, speaking, and acting. You can be assured that they are well aware of what is going on with their money. You are going to find another tracking challenge in this chapter. Just as you tracked your time earlier, you will be tracking your money in this chapter. If you don't know how to handle your own money, how in the world do you expect to handle a business's money? You will trick that off just like you do your time if you don't get a handle on it. Many of you are probably just as wasteful with your money as you are with your time. Unfortunately, the

United States is a wasteful country, so, partly, we can blame your programming. However, now you are with me, and I am going to shake you up till you wake up! The following activities will be found in Chapter Six:

- Accounting Activities: Balance Sheet, Cost of Goods Sold, and Income Statement
- Revenue Model
- Start-Up Costs
- Price Strategies
- Break-Even Point
- Crowdfunding
- Money Tracking Challenge

Chapter Seven is Leadership and Ethics. This chapter is near and dear to my heart. I am in the business of building up leaders. That is what leadership is all about. I am also very firm on my ethical standards and believe that the more ethical you are, the more successful you will be. Sure, you can get somewhere by doing dirty work, but eventually, it will catch up to you. I have seen it happen time and time again. There are a thousand and one cases in this world of ethical wrongdoings. Sure, those people had a nice run and lived a lavish lifestyle, but now they are either dead or rotting in prison. The short game will make you think it is the best game, but it is not. As an Empowered Entrepreneur, you must know you are in the long game to succeed, and in the long game, you must be not only a leader, you must also be ethical. The following activities will be found in Chapter Seven:

- Situational Leadership
- Transformational Leadership
- Self-Analysis Leadership Survey
- Ethical Dilemma Case Study

Chapter Eight is Human Resources. As an Empowered Entrepreneur, you will find out quickly that you are not a lone wolf production. You are going to need a solid team of people to help you run your business. If you plan to grow, you will not be able to do that alone. The Human Resource portion of running a business is probably one of the hardest. Dealing with humans is not an easy job. This is another part that you what not only spend a nice amount of time on, but you will also need to do a lot of good research. I even advise speaking with HR professionals and doing informational interviews, asking them a series of questions. The following activities will be found in Chapter Eight:

- Top 21st Century Skills
- Creating a New Hire Packet and Employee Handbook
- Creating an Onboarding Process

Chapter Nine is Launch, Manage, and Grow. This chapter is a final capstone before the 10 Core Palumbo Principles are given and you are on your way out the door. My hope is that by this point, you are already feeling your empowerment growing. You will have done the bulk of the planning and developing. You will have dug deep inside yourself, and hopefully you will be embracing all your beautiful talents and becoming more excited about your future. You will see there a lot of activities for this chapter as well. All of which will be very beneficial to you as you move forward in being an Empowered Entrepreneur. The following activities will be found in Chapter Nine:

- Step-By-Step Process on How to File for a DBA, EIN, and DUNS
- Insurance Search
- Business Bank Account
- Understanding Your Taxes

Chapter Ten is The 10 Core Palumbo Principles. I will now leave you with my final 10 Core Palumbo Principles. My wisdom. I would encourage you to read this chapter several times. Remember, the gift I give you is the tools to find yourself. Once you have that gift, everything else will fall into place. Please do not rush through the final activities. Spend time on each of them. I promise you they are powerful, and they hold not only healing but freedom, both of which come in pieces. The following activities will be found in Chapter Ten:

- Empowerment Statement
- BVIG's
- Final Challenge: Legacy Letter

Now that you have a better understanding of how the companion workbook is constructed, let's dive into our first challenge: tracking your time. Then remember to start using the planner and scheduling your time. Remember, you have the right to your no. Multitasking only causes procrastination. Space we can recover, but time we cannot. Let's not lose any more to our madness, and let's become EMPOWERED!

On the next page, you will find your tracking challenge. You will track your time for one week. You will write what the day of the week it is and what the date is. Then you will write your start and stop times and indicate what you were doing during those times. You need to be honest. This challenge is to help you grow. You can reflect daily on the time you have tracked, or you can reflect at the end once you have tracked your time for a full week. What you want to do is see how you are spending your time and then make the necessary adjustments so you can use your time better. There will be space for you to write your reflection at the end of the tracking sheets. This challenge will be very eye-opening if you are true to it. Remember, this is to help you grow.

Entrepreneurship Empowered Challenge One: Track Your Time

Day of the Week	Date	Task/Activity (what did you do during this time)
Start Time	Stop Time	
Start Time	Stop Time	
Start Time	Stop Time	
Start Time	Stop Time	
Start Time	Stop Time	
Start Time	Stop Time	
Start Time	Stop Time	
Start Time	Stop Time	
Start Time	Stop Time	
Start Time	Stop Time	
Start Time	Stop Time	
Start Time	Stop Time	
Start Time	Stop Time	
Start Time	Stop Time	
Start Time	Stop Time	
Start Time	Stop Time	
Start Time	Stop Time	
Start Time	Stop Time	

Day of the Week	Date	Task/Activity (what did you do during this time)
Start Time	Stop Time	
Start Time	Stop Time	
Start Time	Stop Time	
Start Time	Stop Time	
Start Time	Stop Time	
Start Time	Stop Time	
Start Time	Stop Time	
Start Time	Stop Time	
Start Time	Stop Time	
Start Time	Stop Time	
Start Time	Stop Time	
Start Time	Stop Time	
Start Time	Stop Time	
Start Time	Stop Time	
Start Time	Stop Time	
Start Time	Stop Time	
Start Time	Stop Time	
Start Time	Stop Time	
Start Time	Stop Time	

Entrepreneurship Empowered Challenge One: Track Your Time

Day of the Week	Date	Task/Activity (what did you do during this time)
Start Time	Stop Time	
Start Time	Stop Time	
Start Time	Stop Time	
Start Time	Stop Time	
Start Time	Stop Time	
Start Time	Stop Time	
Start Time	Stop Time	
Start Time	Stop Time	
Start Time	Stop Time	
Start Time	Stop Time	
Start Time	Stop Time	
Start Time	Stop Time	
Start Time	Stop Time	
Start Time	Stop Time	
Start Time	Stop Time	
Start Time	Stop Time	
Start Time	Stop Time	
Start Time	Stop Time	

Day of the Week	Date	Task/Activity (what did you do during this time)
Start Time	Stop Time	
Start Time	Stop Time	
Start Time	Stop Time	
Start Time	Stop Time	
Start Time	Stop Time	
Start Time	Stop Time	
Start Time	Stop Time	
Start Time	Stop Time	
Start Time	Stop Time	
Start Time	Stop Time	
Start Time	Stop Time	
Start Time	Stop Time	
Start Time	Stop Time	
Start Time	Stop Time	
Start Time	Stop Time	
Start Time	Stop Time	
Start Time	Stop Time	
Start Time	Stop Time	
Start Time	Stop Time	

Entrepreneurship Empowered Challenge One: Track Your Time

Day of the Week	Date	Task/Activity (what did you do during this time)
Start Time	Stop Time	
Start Time	Stop Time	
Start Time	Stop Time	
Start Time	Stop Time	
Start Time	Stop Time	
Start Time	Stop Time	
Start Time	Stop Time	
Start Time	Stop Time	
Start Time	Stop Time	
Start Time	Stop Time	
Start Time	Stop Time	
Start Time	Stop Time	
Start Time	Stop Time	
Start Time	Stop Time	
Start Time	Stop Time	
Start Time	Stop Time	
Start Time	Stop Time	
Start Time	Stop Time	
Start Time	Stop Time	

Day of the Week	Date	Task/Activity (what did you do during this time)
Start Time	Stop Time	
Start Time	Stop Time	
Start Time	Stop Time	
Start Time	Stop Time	
Start Time	Stop Time	
Start Time	Stop Time	
Start Time	Stop Time	
Start Time	Stop Time	
Start Time	Stop Time	
Start Time	Stop Time	
Start Time	Stop Time	
Start Time	Stop Time	
Start Time	Stop Time	
Start Time	Stop Time	
Start Time	Stop Time	
Start Time	Stop Time	
Start Time	Stop Time	
Start Time	Stop Time	
Start Time	Stop Time	

Entrepreneurship Empowered Challenge One: Track Your Time

Day of the Week	Date	Task/Activity (what did you do during this time)
Start Time	Stop Time	
Start Time	Stop Time	
Start Time	Stop Time	
Start Time	Stop Time	
Start Time	Stop Time	
Start Time	Stop Time	
Start Time	Stop Time	
Start Time	Stop Time	
Start Time	Stop Time	
Start Time	Stop Time	
Start Time	Stop Time	
Start Time	Stop Time	
Start Time	Stop Time	
Start Time	Stop Time	
Start Time	Stop Time	
Start Time	Stop Time	
Start Time	Stop Time	
Start Time	Stop Time	
Start Time	Stop Time	

Day of the Week	Date	Task/Activity (what did you do during this time)
Start Time	Stop Time	
Start Time	Stop Time	
Start Time	Stop Time	
Start Time	Stop Time	
Start Time	Stop Time	
Start Time	Stop Time	
Start Time	Stop Time	
Start Time	Stop Time	
Start Time	Stop Time	
Start Time	Stop Time	
Start Time	Stop Time	
Start Time	Stop Time	
Start Time	Stop Time	
Start Time	Stop Time	
Start Time	Stop Time	
Start Time	Stop Time	
Start Time	Stop Time	
Start Time	Stop Time	
Start Time	Stop Time	

Entrepreneurship Empowered Challenge One: Track Your Time

Day of the Week	Date	Task/Activity (what did you do during this time)
Start Time	Stop Time	
Start Time	Stop Time	
Start Time	Stop Time	
Start Time	Stop Time	
Start Time	Stop Time	
Start Time	Stop Time	
Start Time	Stop Time	
Start Time	Stop Time	
Start Time	Stop Time	
Start Time	Stop Time	
Start Time	Stop Time	
Start Time	Stop Time	
Start Time	Stop Time	
Start Time	Stop Time	
Start Time	Stop Time	
Start Time	Stop Time	
Start Time	Stop Time	
Start Time	Stop Time	
Start Time	Stop Time	

Reflection: _____

_____

_____

_____

_____

_____

_____

_____

_____

_____

_____

_____

_____

_____

Entrepreneurship Empowered Planner
Month _____ Year _____

Mon.	Tues.	Wed.	Thurs.	Fri.	Sat.	Sun.
Date	Date	Date	Date	Date	Date	Date
Date	Date	Date	Date	Date	Date	Date
Date	Date	Date	Date	Date	Date	Date
Date	Date	Date	Date	Date	Date	Date
Date	Date	Date	Date	Date	Date	Date

Affirmation:

_____

_____

_____

Goals: _____

_____

_____

_____

How it is going to feel to accomplish these goals: _____

_____

_____

Actionable steps needed to accomplish these goals: _____

_____

_____

_____

_____

_____

Entrepreneurship Empowered Weekly Schedule

Time	Mon. Date	Tues. Date	Wed. Date
7:00am			
7:30am			
8:00am			
8:30am			
9:00am			
9:30am			
10:00am			
10:30am			
11:00am			
11:30am			
12:00pm			
12:30pm			
1:00pm			
1:30pm			
2:00pm			
2:30pm			
3:00pm			
3:30pm			
4:00pm			
4:30pm			
5:00pm			
5:30pm			
6:00pm			
6:30pm			
7:00pm			
7:30pm			
8:00pm			
9:00pm			
10:00pm			

Notes: _____

_____

_____

_____

Entrepreneurship Empowered Weekly Schedule

Thurs. Date	Fri. Date	Sat. Date
		Sun. Date

Notes:

Entrepreneurship Empowered Weekly Schedule

Time	Mon. Date	Tues. Date	Wed. Date
7:00am			
7:30am			
8:00am			
8:30am			
9:00am			
9:30am			
10:00am			
10:30am			
11:00am			
11:30am			
12:00pm			
12:30pm			
1:00pm			
1:30pm			
2:00pm			
2:30pm			
3:00pm			
3:30pm			
4:00pm			
4:30pm			
5:00pm			
5:30pm			
6:00pm			
6:30pm			
7:00pm			
7:30pm			
8:00pm			
9:00pm			
10:00pm			

Notes:

Entrepreneurship Empowered Weekly Schedule

Thurs. Date	*Fri. Date*	*Sat. Date*
		Sun. Date

Notes:

Entrepreneurship Empowered Weekly Schedule

Time	Mon. Date	Tues. Date	Wed. Date
7:00am			
7:30am			
8:00am			
8:30am			
9:00am			
9:30am			
10:00am			
10:30am			
11:00am			
11:30am			
12:00pm			
12:30pm			
1:00pm			
1:30pm			
2:00pm			
2:30pm			
3:00pm			
3:30pm			
4:00pm			
4:30pm			
5:00pm			
5:30pm			
6:00pm			
6:30pm			
7:00pm			
7:30pm			
8:00pm			
9:00pm			
10:00pm			

Notes:

_____

_____

_____

Entrepreneurship Empowered Weekly Schedule

Thurs. Date	Fri. Date	Sat. Date
		Sun. Date

Notes:

_____

_____

_____

_____

Entrepreneurship Empowered Weekly Schedule

Time	Mon. Date	Tues. Date	Wed. Date
7:00am			
7:30am			
8:00am			
8:30am			
9:00am			
9:30am			
10:00am			
10:30am			
11:00am			
11:30am			
12:00pm			
12:30pm			
1:00pm			
1:30pm			
2:00pm			
2:30pm			
3:00pm			
3:30pm			
4:00pm			
4:30pm			
5:00pm			
5:30pm			
6:00pm			
6:30pm			
7:00pm			
7:30pm			
8:00pm			
9:00pm			
10:00pm			

Notes:

Entrepreneurship Empowered Weekly Schedule

Thurs. Date	Fri. Date	Sat. Date
		Sun. Date

Notes:
_____

_____

_____

_____

Entrepreneurship Empowered Weekly Schedule

Time	Mon. Date	Tues. Date	Wed. Date
7:00am			
7:30am			
8:00am			
8:30am			
9:00am			
9:30am			
10:00am			
10:30am			
11:00am			
11:30am			
12:00pm			
12:30pm			
1:00pm			
1:30pm			
2:00pm			
2:30pm			
3:00pm			
3:30pm			
4:00pm			
4:30pm			
5:00pm			
5:30pm			
6:00pm			
6:30pm			
7:00pm			
7:30pm			
8:00pm			
9:00pm			
10:00pm			

Notes:

_____

_____

_____

_____

Entrepreneurship Empowered Weekly Schedule

Thurs. Date	Fri. Date	Sat. Date
		Sun. Date

Notes:

_____

_____

_____

Entrepreneurship Empowered Planner
Month _____ Year _____

Mon.	Tues.	Wed.	Thurs.	Fri.	Sat.	Sun.
Date	Date	Date	Date	Date	Date	Date
Date	Date	Date	Date	Date	Date	Date
Date	Date	Date	Date	Date	Date	Date
Date	Date	Date	Date	Date	Date	Date
Date	Date	Date	Date	Date	Date	Date

Affirmation: _____

_____

_____

_____

Goals: _____

_____

_____

_____

_____

How it is going to feel to accomplish these goals: _____

_____

_____

Actionable steps needed to accomplish these goals: _____

_____

_____

_____

_____

_____

_____

Entrepreneurship Empowered Weekly Schedule

Time	Mon. Date	Tues. Date	Wed. Date
7:00am			
7:30am			
8:00am			
8:30am			
9:00am			
9:30am			
10:00am			
10:30am			
11:00am			
11:30am			
12:00pm			
12:30pm			
1:00pm			
1:30pm			
2:00pm			
2:30pm			
3:00pm			
3:30pm			
4:00pm			
4:30pm			
5:00pm			
5:30pm			
6:00pm			
6:30pm			
7:00pm			
7:30pm			
8:00pm			
9:00pm			
10:00pm			

Notes:

Entrepreneurship Empowered Weekly Schedule

Thurs. Date	*Fri. Date*	*Sat. Date*
		Sun. Date

Notes:

Entrepreneurship Empowered Weekly Schedule

Time	Mon. Date	Tues. Date	Wed. Date
7:00am			
7:30am			
8:00am			
8:30am			
9:00am			
9:30am			
10:00am			
10:30am			
11:00am			
11:30am			
12:00pm			
12:30pm			
1:00pm			
1:30pm			
2:00pm			
2:30pm			
3:00pm			
3:30pm			
4:00pm			
4:30pm			
5:00pm			
5:30pm			
6:00pm			
6:30pm			
7:00pm			
7:30pm			
8:00pm			
9:00pm			
10:00pm			

Notes: _____

_____

_____

_____

Entrepreneurship Empowered Weekly Schedule

Thurs. Date	Fri. Date	Sat. Date
		Sun. Date

Notes:

_____

_____

_____

_____

Entrepreneurship Empowered Weekly Schedule

Time	Mon. Date	Tues. Date	Wed. Date
7:00am			
7:30am			
8:00am			
8:30am			
9:00am			
9:30am			
10:00am			
10:30am			
11:00am			
11:30am			
12:00pm			
12:30pm			
1:00pm			
1:30pm			
2:00pm			
2:30pm			
3:00pm			
3:30pm			
4:00pm			
4:30pm			
5:00pm			
5:30pm			
6:00pm			
6:30pm			
7:00pm			
7:30pm			
8:00pm			
9:00pm			
10:00pm			

Notes:

Entrepreneurship Empowered Weekly Schedule

Thurs. Date	*Fri. Date*	*Sat. Date*
		Sun. Date

Notes:

Entrepreneurship Empowered Weekly Schedule

Time	Mon. Date	Tues. Date	Wed. Date
7:00am			
7:30am			
8:00am			
8:30am			
9:00am			
9:30am			
10:00am			
10:30am			
11:00am			
11:30am			
12:00pm			
12:30pm			
1:00pm			
1:30pm			
2:00pm			
2:30pm			
3:00pm			
3:30pm			
4:00pm			
4:30pm			
5:00pm			
5:30pm			
6:00pm			
6:30pm			
7:00pm			
7:30pm			
8:00pm			
9:00pm			
10:00pm			

Notes:

_____

_____

_____

_____

Entrepreneurship Empowered Weekly Schedule

Thurs. Date	Fri. Date	Sat. Date
		Sun. Date

Notes:

_____

_____

_____

_____

Entrepreneurship Empowered Weekly Schedule

Time	Mon. Date	Tues. Date	Wed. Date
7:00am			
7:30am			
8:00am			
8:30am			
9:00am			
9:30am			
10:00am			
10:30am			
11:00am			
11:30am			
12:00pm			
12:30pm			
1:00pm			
1:30pm			
2:00pm			
2:30pm			
3:00pm			
3:30pm			
4:00pm			
4:30pm			
5:00pm			
5:30pm			
6:00pm			
6:30pm			
7:00pm			
7:30pm			
8:00pm			
9:00pm			
10:00pm			

Notes: _____

_____

_____

_____

Entrepreneurship Empowered Weekly Schedule

Thurs. Date	*Fri. Date*	*Sat. Date*
		Sun. Date

Notes:
_____

_____

_____

_____

Entrepreneurship Empowered Planner
Month _____ Year _____

Mon.	Tues.	Wed.	Thurs.	Fri.	Sat.	Sun.
Date	Date	Date	Date	Date	Date	Date
Date	Date	Date	Date	Date	Date	Date
Date	Date	Date	Date	Date	Date	Date
Date	Date	Date	Date	Date	Date	Date
Date	Date	Date	Date	Date	Date	Date

Affirmation:

_____
_____
_____

Goals:

_____
_____
_____
_____

How it is going to feel to accomplish these goals: _____

_____
_____

Actionable steps needed to accomplish these goals: _____

_____
_____
_____
_____
_____
_____

Entrepreneurship Empowered Weekly Schedule

Time	Mon. Date	Tues. Date	Wed. Date
7:00am			
7:30am			
8:00am			
8:30am			
9:00am			
9:30am			
10:00am			
10:30am			
11:00am			
11:30am			
12:00pm			
12:30pm			
1:00pm			
1:30pm			
2:00pm			
2:30pm			
3:00pm			
3:30pm			
4:00pm			
4:30pm			
5:00pm			
5:30pm			
6:00pm			
6:30pm			
7:00pm			
7:30pm			
8:00pm			
9:00pm			
10:00pm			

Notes:

Entrepreneurship Empowered Weekly Schedule

Thurs. Date	*Fri. Date*	*Sat. Date*
		Sun. Date

Notes:

_____

_____

_____

_____

Entrepreneurship Empowered Weekly Schedule

Time	Mon. Date	Tues. Date	Wed. Date
7:00am			
7:30am			
8:00am			
8:30am			
9:00am			
9:30am			
10:00am			
10:30am			
11:00am			
11:30am			
12:00pm			
12:30pm			
1:00pm			
1:30pm			
2:00pm			
2:30pm			
3:00pm			
3:30pm			
4:00pm			
4:30pm			
5:00pm			
5:30pm			
6:00pm			
6:30pm			
7:00pm			
7:30pm			
8:00pm			
9:00pm			
10:00pm			

Notes:

_____

_____

_____

_____

Entrepreneurship Empowered Weekly Schedule

Thurs. Date	Fri. Date	Sat. Date
		Sun. Date

Notes: _____

_____

_____

Entrepreneurship Empowered Weekly Schedule

Time	Mon. Date	Tues. Date	Wed. Date
7:00am			
7:30am			
8:00am			
8:30am			
9:00am			
9:30am			
10:00am			
10:30am			
11:00am			
11:30am			
12:00pm			
12:30pm			
1:00pm			
1:30pm			
2:00pm			
2:30pm			
3:00pm			
3:30pm			
4:00pm			
4:30pm			
5:00pm			
5:30pm			
6:00pm			
6:30pm			
7:00pm			
7:30pm			
8:00pm			
9:00pm			
10:00pm			

Notes:

Entrepreneurship Empowered Weekly Schedule

Thurs. Date	*Fri. Date*	*Sat. Date*
		Sun. Date

Notes:

Entrepreneurship Empowered Weekly Schedule

Time	Mon. Date	Tues. Date	Wed. Date
7:00am			
7:30am			
8:00am			
8:30am			
9:00am			
9:30am			
10:00am			
10:30am			
11:00am			
11:30am			
12:00pm			
12:30pm			
1:00pm			
1:30pm			
2:00pm			
2:30pm			
3:00pm			
3:30pm			
4:00pm			
4:30pm			
5:00pm			
5:30pm			
6:00pm			
6:30pm			
7:00pm			
7:30pm			
8:00pm			
9:00pm			
10:00pm			

Notes:

Entrepreneurship Empowered Weekly Schedule

Thurs. Date	Fri. Date	Sat. Date
		Sun. Date

Notes:

_____

_____

_____

Entrepreneurship Empowered Weekly Schedule

Time	Mon. Date	Tues. Date	Wed. Date
7:00am			
7:30am			
8:00am			
8:30am			
9:00am			
9:30am			
10:00am			
10:30am			
11:00am			
11:30am			
12:00pm			
12:30pm			
1:00pm			
1:30pm			
2:00pm			
2:30pm			
3:00pm			
3:30pm			
4:00pm			
4:30pm			
5:00pm			
5:30pm			
6:00pm			
6:30pm			
7:00pm			
7:30pm			
8:00pm			
9:00pm			
10:00pm			

Notes:

Entrepreneurship Empowered Weekly Schedule

Thurs. Date	_Fri. Date_	_Sat. Date_
		Sun. Date

Notes:

Entrepreneurship Empowered Planner
Month _____ Year _____

Mon.	Tues.	Wed.	Thurs.	Fri.	Sat.	Sun.
Date	Date	Date	Date	Date	Date	Date
Date	Date	Date	Date	Date	Date	Date
Date	Date	Date	Date	Date	Date	Date
Date	Date	Date	Date	Date	Date	Date
Date	Date	Date	Date	Date	Date	Date

Affirmation:

_____

_____

_____

_____

Goals:

_____

_____

_____

_____

How it is going to feel to accomplish these goals:

_____

_____

Actionable steps needed to accomplish these goals:

_____

_____

_____

_____

_____

_____

Entrepreneurship Empowered Weekly Schedule

Time	Mon. Date	Tues. Date	Wed. Date
7:00am			
7:30am			
8:00am			
8:30am			
9:00am			
9:30am			
10:00am			
10:30am			
11:00am			
11:30am			
12:00pm			
12:30pm			
1:00pm			
1:30pm			
2:00pm			
2:30pm			
3:00pm			
3:30pm			
4:00pm			
4:30pm			
5:00pm			
5:30pm			
6:00pm			
6:30pm			
7:00pm			
7:30pm			
8:00pm			
9:00pm			
10:00pm			

Notes:

_____

_____

_____

_____

Entrepreneurship Empowered Weekly Schedule

Thurs. Date	Fri. Date	Sat. Date
		Sun. Date

Notes:

Entrepreneurship Empowered Weekly Schedule

Time	Mon. Date	Tues. Date	Wed. Date
7:00am			
7:30am			
8:00am			
8:30am			
9:00am			
9:30am			
10:00am			
10:30am			
11:00am			
11:30am			
12:00pm			
12:30pm			
1:00pm			
1:30pm			
2:00pm			
2:30pm			
3:00pm			
3:30pm			
4:00pm			
4:30pm			
5:00pm			
5:30pm			
6:00pm			
6:30pm			
7:00pm			
7:30pm			
8:00pm			
9:00pm			
10:00pm			

Notes: _____

_____

_____

_____

Entrepreneurship Empowered Weekly Schedule

Thurs. Date	Fri. Date	Sat. Date
		Sun. Date

Notes: _____

_____

_____

_____

Entrepreneurship Empowered Weekly Schedule

Time	Mon. Date	Tues. Date	Wed. Date
7:00am			
7:30am			
8:00am			
8:30am			
9:00am			
9:30am			
10:00am			
10:30am			
11:00am			
11:30am			
12:00pm			
12:30pm			
1:00pm			
1:30pm			
2:00pm			
2:30pm			
3:00pm			
3:30pm			
4:00pm			
4:30pm			
5:00pm			
5:30pm			
6:00pm			
6:30pm			
7:00pm			
7:30pm			
8:00pm			
9:00pm			
10:00pm			

Notes:

Entrepreneurship Empowered Weekly Schedule

Thurs. Date	Fri. Date	Sat. Date
		Sun. Date

Notes:

_____

_____

_____

_____

Entrepreneurship Empowered Weekly Schedule

Time	Mon. Date	Tues. Date	Wed. Date
7:00am			
7:30am			
8:00am			
8:30am			
9:00am			
9:30am			
10:00am			
10:30am			
11:00am			
11:30am			
12:00pm			
12:30pm			
1:00pm			
1:30pm			
2:00pm			
2:30pm			
3:00pm			
3:30pm			
4:00pm			
4:30pm			
5:00pm			
5:30pm			
6:00pm			
6:30pm			
7:00pm			
7:30pm			
8:00pm			
9:00pm			
10:00pm			

Notes:

Entrepreneurship Empowered Weekly Schedule

Thurs. Date	Fri. Date	Sat. Date
		Sun. Date

Notes:

Entrepreneurship Empowered Weekly Schedule

Time	Mon. Date	Tues. Date	Wed. Date
7:00am			
7:30am			
8:00am			
8:30am			
9:00am			
9:30am			
10:00am			
10:30am			
11:00am			
11:30am			
12:00pm			
12:30pm			
1:00pm			
1:30pm			
2:00pm			
2:30pm			
3:00pm			
3:30pm			
4:00pm			
4:30pm			
5:00pm			
5:30pm			
6:00pm			
6:30pm			
7:00pm			
7:30pm			
8:00pm			
9:00pm			
10:00pm			

Notes: _____

_____

_____

_____

Entrepreneurship Empowered Weekly Schedule

Thurs. Date	*Fri. Date*	*Sat. Date*
		Sun. Date

Notes:

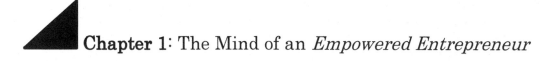

Chapter 1: The Mind of an *Empowered Entrepreneur*

"Once your mindset changes, everything on the outside will change along with it."

—Steve Maraboli, author

The mind of an Empowered Entrepreneur is much different than the average mind. We think very differently. It is our mind that is the one common theme. Sure, we have similar characteristics—and I even provide you with several of them in my book—but it is the mind that makes you not only an Empowered Entrepreneur, but also an Empowered individual. We have a growth mindset, an entrepreneurial mindset, which is one that sees opportunity when others see roadblocks. One that knows with hard work and dedication, no matter how many times I fail or fall on my face, I will rise again. We understand that we have the power to create our future; we do not predict it. We understand that we don't need to control the future because, by doing so, we only create stress. We understand the power of the mind. We know that what we create will come to pass if we faint not. Chapter One is dedicated to personal self-discovery. You are going to go through a series of activities that are going to ask you to take a good look at your mind. You are going to need to be honest with your answers because that is the only way you can grow. We are always growing. We never arrive, you understand, never. Personal growth should be pursued unto death. Meaning, you are in the long game. This is a marathon, not a sprint. There really is no finish line. You see, old ceilings become new floors. Are you ready to be EMPOWERED? If so, let's begin.

Chapter 1, Activity 1: Fixed/Growth Mindset

Please answer the following questions and be truthful with yourself. This is just for you. After you have answered the questions, you will need to tally your score. Your score will indicate if you have a growth mindset or a fixed mindset. Let's give it a try. Circle the answer and add up your points on the space provided.

1. Your intellect is something you are not able to change. You are either smart or you are not.
    a. Strongly Agree   0
    b. Agree   1
    c. Disagree   ②
    d. Strongly Disagree 3

2. Intelligence can always be improved, no matter how much you have.
    a. Strongly Agree   3
    b. Agree   2
    c. Disagree   1
    d. Strongly Disagree 0

3. You are either born with talents (like playing a sport or being musically inclined), or you just don't have any.
   - a. Strongly Agree   0
   - b. Agree   1
   - c. Disagree   2
   - d. Strongly Disagree 3

4. The harder you work, the better you will become.
   - a. Strongly Agree   3
   - b. Agree   2
   - c. Disagree   1
   - d. Strongly Disagree 0

5. When feedback is given to you, you often get upset.
   - a. Strongly Agree   0
   - b. Agree   1
   - c. Disagree   2
   - d. Strongly Disagree 3

6. When feedback is given to you, you appreciate it and take it to heart.
   - a. Strongly Agree   3
   - b. Agree   2
   - c. Disagree   1
   - d. Strongly Disagree 0

7. When you are smart, you don't need to try as hard as others.
   - a. Strongly Agree   0
   - b. Agree   1
   - c. Disagree   2
   - d. Strongly Disagree 3

8. Regardless of whether you are smart or not, you must work hard.
   - a. Strongly Agree   3
   - b. Agree   2
   - c. Disagree   1
   - d. Strongly Disagree 0

9. We are who we are and there is no changing it.
   - a. Strongly Agree   0
   - b. Agree   1
   - c. Disagree   2
   - d. Strongly Disagree 3

10. Because I know I am always growing, I am always willing to learn new things and be open to new experiences.
    - a. Strongly Agree   3
    - b. Agree   2

c. Disagree   1
d. Strongly Disagree 0

Now that you have answered all the questions, go ahead and add up what your total number is. This is your score_____2|_____. The higher your score is, the more of a growth mindset you have. The lower your score is, the more of a fixed mindset you have. Now, let's take some time to think about what you have discovered. If you have a growth or fixed mindset, how did you get to this type of mindset? Did you see it in others? Do your parents or someone close to you have this type of mindset? What experiences in your life helped create the mindset you currently have? Just allow yourself the space to freely write what comes. Then, move on to the next activity. After you finish the next activity, I am going to provide you with some tips that will help you further develop your mind, and when you put them into practice, you will be one step closer to being EMPOWERED! Remember, the way out is within.

Nothing has ever come easy to me and I've always had to work hard to get results. I do believe I have some innate physical abilities but I always have to work hard to make them shine above others.

I am pretty shy & I would say an introvert. In my current position I have had to overcome my fears in order to grow and today I feel more confident about myself and my ability to be respected in my field as a chef and a woman. I think that what I've had to overcome in my personal life, moving to the US, leaving my family back in Italy, coming out of the closet, shows that I am resilient, adaptable & willing to sacrifice a lot for what I want.

My growth mindset has brought me to this point in my life but I want more for myself and I will keep on pushing!!

Chapter 1, Activity 2: What Does Your Mind Say About You?

There is a textbook that I use from time to time called *Entrepreneurship: The Practice and Mindset* by Heidi M. Neck, Christopher P. Neck, and Emma L. Murray. The following mindset activity is derived from that book.[2] What does your mindset really say about you? I would like you to go to a place you haven't been to before. It can be a park, a restaurant, a library, really just about anywhere. It just needs to be unfamiliar. Take this book and a pen with you. I have provided space for you to write. For about five to ten minutes, I want you to look around. Gather your thoughts about what you see. You are now going to write your observations. You will use adjectives to describe what you see. For example, you may see a play structure at the park, but you need to describe it in detail. It may be shiny, empty, curved, broken, rusty, et cetera. You may then see a squirrel in the park. Is it cute, furry, ugly, mean, friendly? After you finish, I want you to sit down and look at the list of words you have before you. Circle all the words that have a positive connotation. Then I want you to put a square around all the words that have a negative connotation.

What is the point of all this, you may ask? The way we see the outside is a direct connection to our mindset. If you see the world as predominantly negative, then your mindset for *Entrepreneurship Empowered* needs to be further developed. If you have a more positive mindset, you will be able to see opportunities and make a difference. What does your mindset say about you? Are you pleased with your mindset? Do you need to work on some areas? Do you struggle with seeing opportunities? I would like to encourage you to change your mindset—doing so will change your life. Below are some tips to help you develop a more positive and growth mindset.

1. Give at least one gratitude every day. The more grateful you are, the more you will attract positive energy to you. The reason you have space provided in your schedule to write an affirmation is because affirmations are powerful. Even if you are just giving gratitude for the air you breathe, that will work. But I want you to dig deep and look around and see how much you really have.

2. Set at least one goal or intention of the day. Nothing too drastic or challenging. Something simple like, "Today I will meditate for five minutes." Or, "Today I will pause and take three deep breaths." Again, nothing too heavy.

3. Take time in the morning and have a morning mirror moment. Take as much or as little time as you need, but practice looking at yourself and finding at least one thing positive to say. Even if it is, "I love you no matter what." The way out is within.

4. I need you to acknowledge your imperfections and embrace them. If you hide them, many times you are only hiding them from yourself. You are only lying to yourself.

5. I want you to fail well. What do I mean? Every day I want you see to any challenge as an opportunity. No longer are you going to allow a challenge to prevent you from gaining even the experience of failing. You will learn so much by failing well because you are going to know that you are not really failing. Rather, you are learning, and the more you try, the better you will get.

6. Get out of the valley of validation and stop wandering in the forest of falsehood. The trees there are only filled with leaves of lies, and the people in the valley are not there. You need to stop seeking approval from anyone right away.

7. When you understand, you have a purpose. You are the value; you need no other to approve of you. There is a big picture, and just like a puzzle when all the pieces come together, "ta-da!" there it will be! You are never to forget that you have a purpose and that you are the value.

8. Always keep in mind that you are growing. Forget about time. It is irrelevant. It is never about how fast you get there as much as it is about the fact that you did arrive at where you were designed to go.

9. Become a researcher of the mind. Specifically, study "brain plasticity."

10. Build up your grit! (We will examine grit in detail later.)

Chapter 1, Activity 3: Self-Awareness Activity

Self-awareness is key to living the EMPOWERED life. You must understand the inner man and work on the inner self in order for your "outer world" to be a true reflection of what you desire. As I told you in the book, the world we live in is a jungle—you either eat or are eaten. It is up to you. I am a LION. But I am not only a LION. I am also a flamingo, a chameleon, and a turtle. I use all four of my animals to their full capacity. I am in constant pursuit of personal development. It really started with dealing with my trauma. You see, the side effects of trauma are nothing nice. If you don't deal with them, they will certainly deal with you. They will affect your entire life. The issue is that many times they have been passed down from generation to generation. Make sure you don't pass it on to your next generation. Break the curse. The way out is within, and I am a living testament that it is possible to overcome. I endured decades upon decades of horrific trauma and then continued to live in a negative headspace where I was attracting more trauma and operating out of side effects. But today I stand before you EMPOWERED, and in my right mind on most good days. Not every day is perfect. I still battle, but I am much healthier now than I have ever been before, and I will continue to grow in health and freedom. As you explore self, many things may arise. I want you to know first and foremost that you are not alone if you are hurting and have dealt with traumatic events. Childhood trauma is very real. Very painful. Young adult trauma is real and very painful. Trauma, period, is real and very painful. There is help for you. You may contact me directly and I will do my very best to provide you with resources that can help you. What I don't want you to do is suffer in silence any longer.

Lao Tzu said, "Knowing others is wisdom, knowing yourself is Enlightenment." I need to know if you are ready to be enlightened. I highly recommend you take the 4 Animals Assessment,[3] which I write about in my book. You will receive a detailed report that will benefit you greatly in all areas of your life. You will even be able to use the information on the report to build your résumé and apply for jobs. You may contact Jesse Ross at www.mrjesseross.com and use the code ProfessorP to access the assessment at a discounted rate. If you take my class at any of the colleges, or if you take my online course, you will be exposed to Jesse Ross and learn more about the 4 Animals. For the self-awareness activity, I want you to spend some time reflecting on self. I want you to write down what you believe your strengths and your weaknesses are. I want you to assess how your emotions are. Are you emotional? Do you cry often or get angry all the time? Are you short-tempered? Do you have mood swings? Do you know your love language? Do you know who you like to be associated with? If you are in one of my college classes, you will take a VARK survey[4] that will tell me what type of leaner you are. This is important information to not only me, but to you. This is how you learn best, and the way we learn is the way we lead. What is your learning style? Are you a morning person, afternoon, or night? Your energy level: When do you work best? Spend some time on how you handle constructive feedback. Are you a people-pleaser? How well are you dealing with others? Do you get along with people, or is there always some type of issue when dealing with others? After you have answered all those questions, I want you to answer the following three questions:

1. What do you want from and/or for your life?
2. What are you willing to start and stop in order to get what you want for and/or from your life?
3. Who is counting on you? (You counting on you counts too.)

Now let's get to reflecting:

1. I want to be my own boss and grow my business to the point where I reach a nice balance between work & home life. My family always comes first!

2. I am willing to stop working for the man & risk my "easy" work life to become successful with my business. I am willing to start looking into myself and trust my instincts & finally take the leap and know that I will be successful. If I fail, I will have learned something greater than anything else, I will have tried my best.

3. My family is counting on me. I do want to take "calculated" risks & not jeopardized what we have built as a family.

Chapter 1, Activity 4: Grit Test

The dice of life will toss you a "no" time and time again. I need you to pick up those dice and shake them, spit on them if you must, and throw them back to this world and say, "My 'YES' is UNDENIABLE!" Grit is passion and perseverance over a long period of time in pursuit of your goals. You need to understand that in order to become an EMPOWERED individual, you must be gritty. Below you will find a grit test. I want you to take the test and see how gritty you are. If you score low, don't worry, by the time you are done working through this workbook and reading *Entrepreneurship Empowered*, you will have grown, and you will be EMPOWERED!

12-Item Grit Scale

Directions for taking the Grit Scale: Please respond to the following items. Be honest. There are no right or wrong answers!

1. I have overcome setbacks to conquer an important challenge.
    a. Very much like me
    (b) Mostly like me 4
    c. Somewhat like me
    d. Not much like me
    e. Not like me at all

2. New ideas and projects sometimes distract me from previous ones.
    a. Very much like me
    b. Mostly like me
    (c) Somewhat like me 3
    d. Not much like me
    e. Not like me at all

3. My interests change from year to year.
    a. Very much like me
    b. Mostly like me
    c. Somewhat like me
    (d) Not much like me 4
    e. Not like me at all

4. Setbacks don't discourage me.
    a. Very much like me
    b. Mostly like me
    (c) Somewhat like me 3
    d. Not much like me
    e. Not like me at all

5. I have been obsessed with a certain idea or project for a short time but later lost interest.*
    a. Very much like me
    (b) Mostly like me 2
    c. Somewhat like me
    d. Not much like me
    e. Not like me at all

6. I am a hard worker.
    (a) Very much like me 5

     b. Mostly like me
     c. Somewhat like me
     d. Not much like me
     e. Not like me at all

7. I often set a goal but later choose to pursue a different one.
     a. Very much like me
     b. Mostly like me
     c. Somewhat like me
     (d) Not much like me 4
     e. Not like me at all

8. I have difficulty maintaining my focus on projects that take more than a few months to complete.
     a. Very much like me
     b. Mostly like me
     c. Somewhat like me
     (d) Not much like me 4
     e. Not like me at all

9. I finish whatever I begin.
     a. Very much like me
     (b) Mostly like me 4
     c. Somewhat like me
     d. Not much like me
     e. Not like me at all

10. I have achieved a goal that took years of work.
     a. Very much like me
     b. Mostly like me
     (c) Somewhat like me 3
     d. Not much like me
     e. Not like me at all

11. I become interested in new pursuits every few months.*
     a. Very much like me
     b. Mostly like me
     c. Somewhat like me
     (d) Not much like me 4
     e. Not like me at all

12. I am diligent.
     a. Very much like me
     (b) Mostly like me 4
     c. Somewhat like me
     d. Not much like me
     e. Not like me at all

Scoring:
1. For questions 1, 4, 6, 9, 10, and 12, assign the following points:
5 = Very much like me
4 = Mostly like me
3 = Somewhat like me
2 = Not much like me
1 = Not like me at all

2. For questions 2, 3, 5, 7, 8, and 11, assign the following points:
1 = Very much like me
2 = Mostly like me
3 = Somewhat like me
4 = Not much like me
5 = Not like me at all

Add up all the points and divide by 12. The maximum score on this scale is 5 (extremely gritty), and the lowest score on this scale is 1 (not at all gritty).

What is your grit score? Reflect a little on the score you have and write what comes to you.

Score 3.66.
I have a tendency to doubt my abilities and trust that my ideas will come to fruition.
I have been successful in my career within limited boundaries but to start from nothing without direc° or limitations is scary to me & I sometimes stop before I start

[5] Duckworth, A.L., Peterson, C., Matthews, M.D., and Kelly, D.R. (2007). Grit: Perseverance and Passion for Long-Term Goals. *Journal of Personality and Social Psychology*. Vol. 92. 1087–1101.

Chapter 1, Activity 4: Creating Your "Why" Statement (also known as your Impact Statement)

Your legacy becomes your "why?" Your "why" drives you from the moment you find it until the moment you leave this earth. Your "why" may slightly change over the years, but more often, it does not. You end up acquiring other "why's" along the way due to your own life metamorphosis. But for right now, I want you to take a few moments to think about your "why." Your "why" is also known as your impact statement. What impact do you desire to have in this world? Your "why" can never be money. It must be something deeper than that. Your "why," along with your divine talents and abilities, will steer you in life and keep you on course. Everyone needs a "why." I am going to share one of mine with you, and then I want you to think about YOUR "why." I have provided space for you to write it out.

"My 'why' is deeply rooted in my desire to help others heal and be free from the trauma they have gone through in their lives. One out of every four girls is abused, and one out of every five boys is abused. I was abused from ages 3–13, then at ages 13–16, I went through another form of abuse. At age 16, I was a freshman in high school and living on my own. This is only a portion of the abuse I endured. One of the greatest callings in my life is to be used to help heal others. I will not only write a book, but I will write multiple books. I will also be speaking on a national and international level. I have many gifts that I plan to use fully. I have learned over time that I have been honored to have to endure what I have and still make it out. Now I give back!"

Now it is your turn. Give it a try. If you need time to think about it, then do that—think. Go to your core. Find your purpose within, and then write out your "why." After you find it, put it up where you can see it. Let it lead you in the direction that you truly desire to go.

My 'why' is rooted in my desire to make people happy with my food inside and out. I believe that food can affect people's mood & emotions but can also help them fight disease & afflictions (obesity diabetes cancer,...). I have been on a healthy eating path & exercising for the last 3 years & I know understand how important it is to control what goes into your body. I have also seen people who wanted to do better with their eating habits struggle with cooking for themselves or the "price tag" of healthy meals. This country's obesity problem is rooted in the inexpensiveness of fast & bad for your body foods. My 'why' is to help people get healthy by sharing my love for food & knowledge through accessible products & cooking classes about nutrition & cooking in general. Home cooked meals can better everything from creating a family time & bound to ensuring quality products are going into your body.

Let's eat to live not live to eat.

Chapter 1, Activity 5: Goal Setting

You should always be setting goals. When you set your goals, you will always need to think about what steps you will need to take in order to accomplish them. I will ask you to set goals several times in this workbook. For this section, the goals I want you to reflect on will be your life goals. What are the things you <u>what</u> for your life? I want you really think and don't hold back. Nothing is impossible. With the right mindset, you can achieve what you set out to achieve. I am living proof of that. Once you understand what you really want for your life, then you will be able to start working on the steps you need to take to accomplish those dreams and life goals. I encourage you as you sit with this activity to take several deep breaths and allow yourself to be in a calm state. You may even wish to meditate and actually see your "self" in the future. There is a future you calling you to your higher self. Think about that. Let that give you encouragement. You may even write yourself a goal letter. Write the letter to yourself, say, in ten years or even twenty years. What do you want to accomplish? What dreams do you wish to see manifested by then? What level of education will you have acquired by then? The questions are endless. Give it a try. Make sure to sign it and date it. Then in the future, you can read what you wrote and see how well you did.

I am turning 40 years old this month & I feel I am running out of time to achieve great goals but ultimately I would like to have a successful business that allows me to do what I love (share my love for food & cooking) while allowing me to spend quality time with my family (my wife & our 2 kids). I want to be a supportive parent & push my kids to reach their goals. I want to be able to travel the world with my wife & visit my family in France more often. I want to be able to give back to the community I live in & better people's lives through great food products

Chapter 1, Activity 6: Creating a Vision Board

Did you know that caterpillars have something called "imaginal cells"? They are cells that are, well, imagined. You see, once the caterpillar has eaten enough food, the new imaginal cells come forward. A new way of thinking begins. This becomes even more apparent after the struggle in the cocoon—the struggle for the caterpillar to morph into the beautiful butterfly it was purposed to be. The caterpillar and the butterfly both have a purpose, as each of us does. No matter what stage we are at in our lives, understanding our purpose is critical to being an Empowered Entrepreneur.

Vision, just like purpose, is critical to *Entrepreneurship Empowered*. You may be surprised at how many major deals close on one fact. The investor can see that the Empowered Entrepreneur is a visionary. When you are a visionary, you bring the extraordinary to life. Your mindset is creative and not limited. Thought that is no longer limited will result in experiences that are no longer limited. The visionary knows this because their thoughts are not limited.

Visionaries are able to manifest. Vision boards are a great way to activate your vision. I have several vision boards. I have seen many things come to fruition through my boards. When I create them, I not only think about the vision, but I have learned how to feel the vision bringing the heart and the mind together. If you are hoping for rain in the desert, you must not just pray for it. You must feel the rain. You must smell the rain. You must be wearing rain gear and be prepared for the rain. This is really the heart of vision—the feeling of it. If you truly want to succeed as an Empowered Entrepreneur, then you need to not only see yourself and your business succeeding, you need to feel it. You need to feel what it is like to wear imported silk suits. You need to feel what it is like to sit at the top of your high-rise office building. The feeling is the part that brings it to life.

Empowered Entrepreneurs do not predict the future—they create it. Your final task in this chapter will be to create a vision board.

There are several ways you can create your vision board. You can gather magazines and cut out pictures and or words. You will need glue sticks and poster board to place the pictures on. You can also use a computer and google different things that represent your vision and then save the pictures. You can then take those pictures and place them in a Word document. You could even create it in Adobe Photoshop. You could use your smartphone (same concept as with a computer). Google the things you desire for yourself, your business, your life, your family, and so on. Then save the pictures to your camera roll. You will then need a collage maker—there are many free apps out there that can make picture collages. Then place whichever pictures you like in the collage. TA-DA! You now have your vision board.

While creating the vision board, you really want to be connected in thought and heart. See yourself in the boat that you just cut out. Feel the breeze as you walk the beach and watch the sunset in the picture of Bali that is now on your board. See the increase in financial freedom and see that you are rich in love, time, talents, and the like. I use a lot of words in my vision boards, as words are my love language. What is your love language? If it is words, then make sure to use lots of positive words on your board.

The vision board needs to be placed where you can see it every day. For the one you did with your phone, you may save it as your lock screen or background screen. You could even send it to be printed as a photograph. For your Word document boards, you can print them out in color, but black and white will do, too. The poster board method is simple: just put that sucker up on your wall. Put them all up on your wall. Look at them. Let them breathe and live within you. Go back to feeling your vision and believing in it. Before you know it, you will be driving the Camaro you put on your board. You will be floating in a hot air balloon ride. You will be walking the streets of Rome. All of what I just listed, from the Camaro to Rome, were on my vision board and have come to reality. I could go on and on, but now I want you to give it a try.

Please remember this one thing: the vision is for an appointed time. Though it may tarry, it will not be late. For everything there is a season. You must be patient and just know that your vision will come to pass if you faint not.

Remember the caterpillar and the imaginal cells I told you about at the beginning of the chapter? We, too, have such cells. They come forward as we transform our lives. Your vision is your imaginal cells. It is your higher purpose. I am sure the caterpillar had its doubts, and I can only imagine its friends and family gave it a hard time. *You're back imagining things, aren't you? You really believe you have a higher purpose? You are so low to the ground that the only thing that has you beat is a snake. Come on now. You think you will really fly one day?* Have you ever been mocked by your friends or family for what you imagined? What you believed your higher power to be? I have, and it hurt. But with the same confidence of a caterpillar that walked so low to the ground, I believed that I had imaginal cells—my higher purpose cells. And at the right time, in the right season, I would go into a very dark place. I would let go of my family, friends, and foes. I would transform, and then I would struggle just a little more. Finally, I would break through the cocoon. The most beautiful imagined butterfly you ever saw in your life.

Now go create your imaginal cells. It is time for you to grow. Healthy things grow. Growing things change. Change is good. You have the power in your mind to be whatever you desire. But faith is dead without work. And so is vision. You must execute. The remaining chapters will provide you with the knowledge and the tools you need to help increase your ability to execute. Before you know it, you will be flying in the air with me.

Create Your Vision Board Here

healthy Body + Soul $\longrightarrow$ healthy eating $\longrightarrow$ Business from Hot Sauce to Booths/Food Truck to Restaurant to GIVE BACK TO MY KIDS + COMMUNITY.

Support for my family. time & Money

TRAVEL THE WORLD JAPAN- PERU- NEW ZEALAND- HAWAii- COSTA RICA

TRAVEL TO FRANCE OFTEN (Family + Friends)

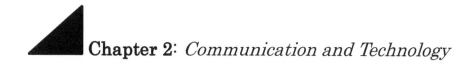

Chapter 2: *Communication and Technology*

"Communication—the human connection—is the key to personal and career success."

—Paul J. Meyer, author and speaker

Communication and Technology go hand in hand, which is why I have looped them together in the same chapter. The activities you will find in this chapter will help you grow both in communication, as well as in digital fluency. I am going to need you to master your communication and understand there is an art to it. The more successful we are in effectively communicating, the better we will do in business and in life. Remember, in this crazy jungle, all the animals speak a different language, and you will need to understand how each one of them speaks. You will need to embrace them in order to understand them. The most important part of effective communication is listening. You will see your first activity will start with that very simple principle. Just listen.

Chapter 2, Activity 1: Effective Communication

One time during the next week, practice "active listening" for five minutes, either with your partner, your child, a friend, or a colleague. Remember to allow the speaker to finish, listen for the content and feelings of the speaker, and validate those feelings. Then come back and reflect on what just took place when you were actively listening. What did you notice from the person you were listening to? Did you hear things differently because you were just listening—listening to understand? Take a moment to reflect and write what comes to you.

_____

_____

_____

_____

_____

_____

_____

_____

_____

_____

_____

_____

_____

Once during the next week, practice speaking up about an issue or problem that has been worrying you. Remember to be positive, be clear and brief, be selective; communicate your feelings, and ask for feedback. Then, after you have done the activity, I want you to come back and reflect on how it went. Did emotions get in the way, or were you able to hold your ground and be emotionally intelligent and logical? Did you feel as though you were heard? Just reflect on how it felt to speak up. Write all that comes to you.

_____

_____

_____

_____

_____

_____

_____

_____

_____

_____

_____

_____

_____
_____
_____
_____
_____
_____
_____
_____
_____
_____
_____
_____
_____
_____
_____
_____
_____
_____
_____
_____
_____
_____
_____
_____
_____

A large portion of our communication is nonverbal. I need you to be as effective with your nonverbal communication as you are with your verbal communication. I need you to make sure you take good care of yourself, that your physical appearance is always clean and presentable. Remember, you don't have to have a lot of money to look nice. Thrift stores have beautiful clothing that is fairly inexpensive, and there are several nonprofit organizations around that have clothes closets where you can obtain free professional clothing.

Chapter 2, Activity 2: Technology and Communication Working Together

Technology and communication are always working together. Technology itself speaks many languages, and I need you to understand as much of it as possible. The more you learn, the better off you will be. This activity is a research activity. I want you to research Microsoft Mobile Office. There are several ways you can use your smartphone to conduct business. In the space provided, I would like for you to write about what you found in your research and then take some time and think about how you will use a mobile office when doing business.

Chapter 2, Activity 3: Becoming More Digitally Fluent

Digital fluency is mission-critical to being an Empowered Entrepreneur. You must understand how to use a computer and software. For this activity, I am going to have you look up some definitions.

Management information system: _____
_____
_____
_____
_____

Computer hardware: _____
_____
_____
_____

Computer software: _____
_____
_____
_____

Intranet: _____
_____
_____
_____

Internet: _____
_____
_____
_____

Network: _____
_____
_____
_____

E-commerce:

Cyber security:

Technology S-curve:

RFID "tags":

Internet marketing:

Quick Response (QR) code:

Additional notes:

Entrepreneurship Empowered Challenge Two: Microsoft Suite Challenge

I am always shocked when my students come to me and have no clue how to use some of the most basic software programs out there. Microsoft Word, PowerPoint, and Excel are mission-critical to everyone in entrepreneurship and business. And because you are an EMPOWERED ENTREPRENEUR, you need to have a basic understanding how to use these programs.

Alison (https://alison.com/course/microsoft-office-2010-revised-2018)[6] is a free web-based educational portal that offers different types of free online courses. For this challenge, you are going to go to the Alison website, and you are going to take the Microsoft Office Course. Space is provided for you to make notes of how you did and what you learned. If you are in my class, you will be asked to submit the certificate that you received upon completion of the course. In a world full of technology, it is sad to see how many people don't know how to use Microsoft Office. I can promise you it is the go-to software system in the business world— not Google Docs.

_____

_____

_____

_____

_____

_____

_____

_____

_____

_____

_____

_____

_____

_____

_____

_____

_____

_____

_____

_____

◤ Chapter 3: *Types of Empowered Entrepreneurs, Business Legal Structure, and Intellectual Property*

"Behind every small business, there's a story worth knowing. All the corner shops in our towns and cities, the restaurants, cleaners, gyms, hair salons, hardware stores—these didn't come out of nowhere."

—Paul Ryan, author

Now we are going to focus our attention on the different types of Empowered Entrepreneurs, the different legal structures for a business, and intellectual property. In the book *Entrepreneurship Empowered*, you will find terms and definitions for the different types of Empowered Entrepreneurs. I suggest you read Chapter Three, then come back to the workbook to do the three activities you will find within.

Chapter 3, Activity 1: Discovering What Type of Empowered Entrepreneur You Are

I want you to think for a moment about which type of Empowered Entrepreneur you believe you are. Does your mind never shut off? Are you always creating, like the serial entrepreneur? Do you need order and structure? If so, perhaps being a franchisee would work best for you. What about simply buying an existing business, how would that suit you? Do you have a heart and a passion for saving the world? Then maybe you are a social entrepreneur. Or do you wish to work inside either a corporation or business and operate in your entrepreneurial gift that way? Take a moment and think. Then, on the lines provided below, write out which Empowered Entrepreneur you believe would work best for you. Knowing this information will be helpful as you move forward.

_____

_____

_____

_____

_____

_____

_____

_____

_____

_____

_____

Chapter 3, Activity 2: Business Legal Structure

Understanding the different legal structures for businesses is one of the most complex parts to learning business. I see time and time again, students struggle to not only understand, but they struggle with knowing which legal structure to select. You must consider all your risks. As a sole proprietor, you are 100% responsible for all liabilities, as you and the business are one. When you are a Limited Liability Company (LLC) or Corporation (C Corp, S Corp), the liability is on the business, not you. You will need your book next to you as you work on this next activity to help you better understand how to structure your business. In this activity, you are going to be given a series of scenarios, and you will need to select the business structure that best fits.

1. John and Ryan have been friends since high school and even attended college together. Ryan graduated with a degree in computer science. John earned a degree in business administration. Both have an interest in computers. They have been helping family and friends since high school with minor computer issues. They notice that in their local town, no one is providing computer services. They each have some savings and are considering going into business. What legal structure should they choose? When choosing that legal structure, what are things they need to consider and have in place? What are the pros and cons of the legal structure chosen?

_____

_____

_____

_____

_____

_____

_____

_____

_____

_____

_____

_____

_____

2. Racheal is a stay-at-home mom. She and her family have successfully eliminated over $60,000 in debt, and she is gifted in what one would call "mom economics." Racheal took a night college class in small business management to explore options for starting her own business. Her college professor encouraged her to build a business based on her removal of debt and her "mom economics." She has low risk and few personal assets but does own a home. In what business legal structure should Rachael form her business? What will she need to do in order to form her business in this

legal structure? What are the pros and cons of forming her business with the legal structure chosen?

_____

_____

_____

_____

_____

_____

_____

_____

_____

_____

_____

_____

3. Margret sells specialized soaps and lotions that she makes in-house. She has a growing client list and a thriving business. She is currently a sole proprietor but feels the need to change her business legal structure. What would you advise her to do? What next legal structure do you believe would be her best fit? What would she need to consider when selecting the chosen legal structure? What are the pros and cons of the chosen structure?

_____

_____

_____

_____

_____

_____

_____

_____

_____

_____

4. Byron owns a family business that was passed down to him from his grandfather. The business, founded in 1959, is a retail paint store that also specializes in window installations. The business started as a sole proprietorship; then, in early 1980, it changed to a limited liability company.

Byron is considering changing the legal structure. The business is thriving, and growth potential is very high. The family already owns three locations, and more are on the horizon. Which legal structure would you advise Byron to choose? What would he need to consider when selecting the chosen legal structure? What are the pros and cons of the chosen structure?

_____

_____

_____

_____

_____

_____

_____

_____

_____

_____

_____

_____

_____

_____

_____

_____

Now I want you to take some time and think about what legal structure would work best for you and your business. I need you to be realistic. If you don't have any assets, what are you really protecting? Remember, as a sole proprietor, you are responsible for all liability. But what really are your risks? You need to carefully consider everything. I encourage you to take time to think and write what comes to you.

_____

_____

_____

_____

_____

_____

_____

_____

_____

Chapter 3, Activity 3: Intellectual Property Search

For this activity, you are going to need your book so that you can read the terms and definitions for each type of intellectual property. You will also need access to the web so you can do a patent and trademark search. First, I want you to do a patent search. You will find the patent and trademark search on the same website: https://www.uspto.gov/.[7] You will go to that website and start with a patent search. Then you will do a trademark search. I also encourage you to read over the information on the site. Explore the site, not just the search option.

1. Patent search: What do you own that you just love? I want you to go to the site and do a patent search on that item. Pay attention to what you find. Read all sections, as there is a lot of information given. Now go and do a search for something related to your business. What did you find? Make sure to note all that you found.

_____

_____

_____

_____

_____

_____

_____

_____

_____

_____

_____

_____

_____

_____

_____

_____

_____

_____

_____

_____

_____

2. Now I want you to do a trademark search. You can trademark words as well as logos. Go do a search again for a product that you know. Nike, for example. Go check out the trademark information on Nike or another brand you love. Then I want you to search a trademark for your business name and see what comes up. Write down all that you find.

_____

_____

_____

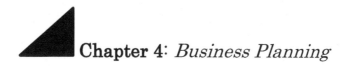 **Chapter 4:** *Business Planning*

"Planning is bringing the future into the present so that you can do something about it now."

—Alan Lakein, author

We are now going to begin our planning phase. This first part is really all about brainstorming and getting what is in our head onto paper, so we can examine it. Remember, no self-censoring. Allow everything to come. You will want to do some research for these activities and see what is out in the market and industry. Look at what is going on in the world. Remember your "why," and always keep in mind that you are figuring out how best to plan your business so it is successful in solving problems. The first activity is something I use in all my general business classes as an in-class exercise. I use it when I teach my students about the business plan. I also give them the real deal, which you will read about in the book. I am not a big fan of the business plan, as I am a new millennium educator and a realist. I am much bigger on the business model, canvas, and pitch deck, which are your second and third activities. I am even bigger on asking other business owners what they have done in regard to business planning, which is why your final activity in this chapter is to do an informational interview on a local business owner.

Chapter 4, Activity 1: Business Planning

Imagine you are preparing to write a business plan for a new company you want to start. Answer the following questions:

What is your business idea? _____

_____

_____

_____

_____

_____

_____

_____

_____

_____

_____

_____

Describe the two most significant barriers you expect to face while launching the business, then explain how you will overcome those obstacles.

Start from (Zero)

No notoriety

What legal structure will you choose for your business? Will you choose to be a sole proprietorship, a partnership, or a corporation? If so, why?

Sole proprietor to start

Who are your major competitors for this business? What are their strengths and weaknesses?

common place Hot Sauce w/ preservatives

→ well-known ⊕
→ preservatives ⊖
→ sugar ⊖

What is your target market for this business? (When a small business starts up, it does not have the resources to market its product to everyone in the world. Therefore, discuss to whom you would market your product. Describe these people in detail—their gender, age, income, education level, ethnicity, personality characteristics, etc.)

How will you determine the price of your product?

based off food cost

What will your pricing strategy be? Will you offer the lowest cost in the industry, or will you offer high quality and unique features in order to justify a higher cost than your competitors?

higher cost - better product you can trust

How will you access the marketplace? Will you advertise (if so, how and where?), attend trade shows, establish a website, open a store? If you open a store, where will it be located?

Farmer's markets
Online

How will you staff and manage your business? For what positions will you hire, and how will you recruit for those positions? Write a job title for each position and include how much you plan to pay these people per year or per hour.

How will you finance your business? Discuss the use of equity and debt. How much are you willing to put into the business? How much debt are you willing to take on?

_____

_____

_____

_____

_____

_____

_____

_____

_____

_____

_____

_____

_____

_____

Control: How will all the activities of the business be monitored in order to ensure success? (For example, you could have sales targets.) What will be the schedule of monitoring? Weekly, monthly, quarterly?

_____

_____

_____

_____

_____

_____

_____

_____

_____

Chapter 4, Activity 2: Business Model Canvas Brainstorming

In your book, you will find the business canvas model and information regarding what it is and how it relates to business planning. For this activity, you are going to take time and think. Please answer each section of the business canvas model.

Customer Value Proposition (CVP)/Offering: (Note: this is your purple cow and what sets you apart from the rest.) What problem are you helping solve for your client or customer?

_____

_____

_____

_____

_____

_____

_____

_____

_____

_____

_____

Customer Segments: Who are your customers? Who are the most important customers? The more detailed you can be with your customer segment, the better you will be able to market to them.

_____

_____

_____

_____

_____

_____

_____

_____

_____

_____

_____

Channels: How are you going to communicate, distribute, and sell to your customers? Which way do they prefer? What are the most cost-effective channels? What are the most time-effective channels?

_____

_____

_____

_____

_____

_____

_____

_____

_____

_____

_____

Customer Relations: What way(s) will you get and keep new customers? How does this strategy fit in with the other parts of the business model?

_____

_____

_____

_____

_____

_____

_____

_____

_____

_____

_____

_____

_____

_____

_____

Key Resources: What do you need in order to offer your CVP?

_____

_____

_____

_____

_____

_____

_____

_____

_____

_____

_____

_____

Key Activities: What will you need to do in order to provide your CVP?

_____

_____

_____

_____

_____

_____

_____

_____

_____

_____

_____

_____

Key Partnerships: Who all will you need in order to deliver on your CVP? Who are your partners and suppliers? What things will you need to outsource to your partners? What resources do you need from your partner? Who is on your team?

_____

_____

_____

_____

_____

_____

_____

_____

_____

_____

_____

Cost Structure: What are all of your costs involved in operating and running your business in order to fulfill your CVP?

_____

_____

_____

_____

_____

_____

_____

_____

_____

_____

_____

_____

_____

_____

Revenue Streams: What are your customers willing to pay? What do they currently pay for solving the problem? How many different revenue streams do you potentially have?

Chapter 4, Activity 3: Pitch Deck Search

The pitch deck is a slide presentation that, many times, is built off of by using the canvas model. It will clearly tell your target audience the key essentials of your business. More importantly, it starts by addressing what the problem is and what solution you have that cures the problem. There are many templates out there to use, and Guy Kawasaki—the gentleman whose quote started off this chapter—is very well known for pitch decks and has several templates to review and use. Right now, google "Guy Kawasaki pitch decks." You are looking for the top ten slides that Guy recommends you need for your pitch deck. I want you to write those ten slides in the space provided below. Also, be sure to note any other suggestions he has for you regarding the presentation. Then, explore the templates he provides, and make sure to save a few for future reference. Take note of design elements, as well as content. This will help you as you develop your own pitch deck.

Chapter 4, Activity 4: Interviewing a Small Business Owner

For your last activity in Chapter Four, you are going to interview a small business owner. Meeting them in person at their place of business is the best, but a phone call will do just fine. I do suggest interviewing someone in your industry. There are plenty of people out there to speak with. You are going to ask them the following questions and, of course, any other questions you feel you would like to know. You never want to take too much of a business owner's time. Always be grateful and give thanks for the opportunity to speak with them.

Name of Business: _____

Owner's Name: _____

Contact Information: _____

_____

What made them go into business? _____

_____

_____

_____

_____

What is their biggest struggle as a business owner? _____

_____

_____

_____

_____

_____

How have they legally structured their business? _____

_____

_____

_____

_____

_____

_____

_____

What advice would they give you (a budding entrepreneur)?

_____

_____

_____

_____

_____

_____

_____

_____

_____

_____

_____

Did they write a business plan?

_____

_____

If they did, then I want you to ask them if it helped them or not.

_____

_____

_____

_____

If they didn't write a business plan, ask them why.

_____

_____

_____

_____

_____

_____

_____

Did they do any planning? If so, what kind?

_____

_____

_____

_____

_____

_____

_____

Additional questions/notes:

_____

_____

_____

_____

_____

_____

_____

_____

_____

_____

_____

_____

_____

_____

_____

_____

_____

_____

Chapter 5: *Marketing and Branding*

"Marketing is no longer about the stuff you sell, but the stories you tell."

—Seth Godin, author and entrepreneur

I absolutely love marketing. I could write an entire book on marketing, and you will find that Chapter Five is one of my meatier chapters. This is true for this workbook, as you will find a lot of activities in this chapter. Don't rush through any of the processes. But especially with marketing, I want you to spend time thinking about, researching, and developing your marketing and branding. Seth Godin hits the nail on the head with the quote above. You are going to become a master storyteller, and everything about your marketing and branding needs to scream your story. Remember that emotional intelligence is deeply tied to marketing. It is why so many powerful brands are so successful in their marketing strategies. If I can get your emotions, I can get your wallet and/or purse. For this chapter, you are going to start with yourself. You are going to find out what your personal brand is, so the very first activity is a personal branding activity and a powerful exercise. Once you understand your personal brand, you will use that to build your business brand and marketing. First, you will do the personal branding activity, exploring emotional intelligence and color psychology. Secondly, you will move on to name creation, which requires you to remove your self-censorship. Thirdly, you will start working on your vision, mission, values, and *ENTREPRENEURSHIP EMPOWERED* SMARTER goals. Following that, you will move into creating a slogan for your business. Finally, you will work on a marketing plan. I encourage you to take your time with the plan and do the research required to make the plan as detailed as possible. I promise you investors will want to see that you have done your due diligence with regard to the marketing plan. Now is your time to do the groundwork to set yourself up for success in the future. I believe that this part of the workbook will be one of your favorite sections.

Chapter 5, Activity 1: Self-Branding Exercise

You are the brand. I want you to ask five to seven people to describe you in three words. Tell them that you will not be upset by what they say if they need to say something that could be a little hard to swallow. You need to know. Tell them not to think very long, but to say whatever three words come to mind. Make sure you write them down. If you see a word pop up more than once, make sure to circle that word. It may happen with a few words. Then you are going to reflect on what you have been told. The words that popped up a few times are your strongest brand traits. Now, do you agree or disagree with the way you were described? Write about it.

How people see you is your brand. You need to be aware of how you are being seen. This final activity is solely dedicated to your personal brand. You will be creating a personal mantra or tagline. A mantra is short and to the point. This mantra is for your life—not for a business, but for you. The next step is to create a logo. Design yourself a personal logo. I am going to provide you with examples of how I did this exercise, and then there will be space provided for you to write your answers. You may also want to use a computer to do the logo work. Or you may draw it. I do suggest, however, if you use a computer, take a printout of the logo you design and glue it into your workbook (just so you keep everything together). My example is provided below.

Self-Branding Assignment example:

- Words that describe me:
    - Creative, Bold, Giving
    - Giving, Passionate, Leader
    - Bold, Driven, Gritty
    - Aggressive, Brave, Creative
    - Strong, Giving, Leader
    - Passionate, Bold, Driven
    - Resilient, Gritty, Giving
        - ➢ I would have to agree with the words that others have used to describe me. I know some of my core strengths are being a leader, being creative, and I love to give. I can be aggressive from time to time, but I would hope others would not be too taken aback by my aggressive traits.
- Mantra/Tagline:
    - Empowered Encourager
    - Logo:

Words that describe me: _____

1. _____
2. _____
3. _____
4. _____
5. _____
6. _____
7. _____

Reflection: _____

_____

_____

_____

_____

_____

_____

_____

_____

_____

_____

_____

Mantra/Slogan: _____

_____

_____

_____

_____

Logo: _____

Chapter 5, Activity 2: Emotional Intelligence and Color Psychology

Emotional intelligence is key to not only being an Empowered Entrepreneur, but also to being Empowered period. For this activity, you are going to do some research. I want you to find two or three articles on emotional intelligence—specifically in marketing. I also want you to check out how color is used. I want you to learn the psychology of color. I am providing you with a website to visit for color psychology.[8] After you have done some research on emotional intelligence, I want you to find an emotional intelligence quiz and take it. See how emotionally intelligent you are. There are plenty of quizzes and assessments on the web for free that you can take. Then, in the space provided, I want you to write about what you found in your research. I also want you to think about how you are going to use emotional intelligence when creating your brand. I also want you to pick a color theme from the color psychology exercise and begin working with those colors as you develop your branding.

Link: https://www.colorpsychology.org/color-psychology-marketing/

Chapter 5, Activity 3: Name Creation

"It's all in a name." Have you ever heard that saying before? Well, it is often true. When you are creating your brand name, you need to be cautious of a few things. First, does someone else already have that name, and are they doing business under that name? You will need to find that out right away. But how do you even come up with a name in the first place? I would encourage you to go to a quiet place, a place that works with your highest element—water, fire, air, or earth. Sit in that quiet place and allow whatever to come to you regarding your business and name. Write down everything that comes. Don't throw anything away at first. Then go back through your list and examine what you have. But don't be too harsh on yourself. Don't judge too much. Just remember a few golden rules.

Have you ever seen the name of a business and thought, *Huh? How do you pronounce that? What does that mean*? You don't want a name that is too confusing, hard to spell, or hard to pronounce. It should not have any underlying message that only you know. It needs to be fresh and timeless because you will want it to be with you the entire time you are in business. Developing a solid brand name is very important. There is power in a name, so choose wisely. Remember, just let everything come to you. After you write all the names that come to you, test your top choices with your target market, family, friends, and the like. See what sticks and what doesn't.

Chapter 5, Activity 4: Vision, Mission, and Value Development with SMARTER Business Goal Setting

As Empowered Entrepreneurs, we do not predict our future; we create it. We have a vision. We understand our mission. We hold true to our values. This activity will help you in developing your vision, mission, and values. Take some time and do some research first. I want you to go to the web to do some searching. Who is your favorite brand or company? I want you to see if you can find their mission, vision, and what values they stand for. Then do a little research on other businesses and brands and see what they have. Then come back and do some developing of your own as it relates to your business.

The marketing strategy process starts with the company vision. The vision of the company addresses the question: "Where is the company going?" It addresses future goals and milestones yet to be accomplished. The mission of the company addresses the following questions: Why does the business exist? What do we do? How do we do it? And for whom do we do it? Both the vision and mission provide direction for the company. Objectives are then set in place, which provides us with the steps of how we are going to get where. We say, "We desire to be..." followed by the steps we must take in order to fulfill our mission. For many years, marketing objectives have been known by an acronym called SMART (i.e., **S**pecific, **M**easurable, **A**chievable, **R**ealistic, and **T**ime-based). But it is a new millennium, and we need to be SMARTER, so I have added two more objectives: **E**xecutable and **R**elevant. In the space provided, I want you to develop your vision, mission, and values. Then I want you to write out what your SMARTER objectives would be in order to accomplish what you have developed.

Chapter 5, Activity 5: Slogan and Hashtag Development

Both slogans and hashtags are effective in building your brand. The hashtag game is something serious. In my book *Entrepreneurship Empowered,* I write about how I have grown my following on Instagram—all by using hashtags. You definitely want to use hashtags in your marketing, especially on Instagram and Twitter, where they work the best. For the first part of this activity, you are going to do some slogan and tagline creating. I have given you some examples of popular slogans/taglines. See if you can figure them out. Then I want you to work on your own tagline. Develop a few and then test the ones you come up with on your target market. See if they like them or not.

Kid Tested. Mother Approved.

Life's Good

Trusted Everywhere

Maybe She's Born With It

We Try Harder

Keep Walking

Gather 'Round the Good Stuff

Makes Mouths Happy

Something Special in the Air

It's Not Just a Job, It's an Adventure!

Now you give it a try. What is your business slogan/tagline going to be?

Chapter 5, Activity 6: Marketing Plan Development

Market research is a super important step. So, how do you begin to do market research? Market research is the gathering of and the interpretation of data in a specific industry. It also includes answers to a series of questions, and more importantly, the developing of your target market. There are two types of data that exist for market research: primary data and secondary data. Primary data is data you develop. You gather the information from doing research, test markets, surveys, focus groups, and so on. Secondary data is data that already exists. The research has been done for you, and the information is published and available for use. There can be a cost associated with some secondary data, but overall, there is an incredible amount of solid secondary data that is available for free. As with any data, please be sure you check your sources. Make sure the sources are legitimate and reputable. Some of the information that you should be able to find out directly from secondary data includes:

- *The total size of your industry*
- *Trends in the industry—is it growing or shrinking?*
- *The total size of your target market and what share is realistic for you to obtain*
- *Trends in the target market—is it growing or shrinking? How are customer needs or preferences changing?*

Below are a few additional questions that you should be able to answer from your research.

- *Who are your customers?*
- *What do they buy now?*
- *Why do they buy?*
- *When do they buy?*
- *What will make them buy from you?*

Who are your customers? This is one of the most important questions to answer. This is also known as your *target market.* I am always reminding my students and clients that they cannot serve everyone, nor do they really want to serve everyone. Even though I do all I can to drill this into their heads, I always receive in my students' business briefs a very large target market. Then I remind them that they must bring in that market and be more focused. The market is broken down into segments. There are several different segments, but according to Active Marketing, an online branding and marketing research company, the list below contains the most common.[9] Remember, you will not choose all of them. You will, however, select some.

- ***Psychographic:*** *Grouping your customers into cultural clusters, social status, lifestyle, and personality type.*
- ***Decision Makers:*** *Grouping your customers based on who decides to purchase your product within the company structure.*
- ***Behavioral:*** *Grouping customers by product usage. For example: light, medium, or heavy users. This stage also factors in brand loyalty and the type of user.*

- *Geographic:* Grouping customers by a specific area, such as regions of the country or state and urban or rural.
- *Distribution:* Grouping customers based on where they go to purchase your product, such as online, a store, or through a catalog.
- *Demographic:* Grouping customers by age, income level, gender, family size, religion, race, nationality, language, etc.

Remember to use the list provided above to help you develop your target market. One of the things you will want to consider is, do you have a product or service that is niche? A niche market is defined as *"a small, more narrowly defined market that is not being served well, or at all, by mainstream product or service marketers."* I have a niche market: I only serve social security and disability lawyers. Because of my niche, I was able to have somewhat of a monopoly in my industry. Niches are wonderful if you have one.

For this activity, you are not only going to create your target market, but you will do market research and competitive analysis. I want you to research who your competitors are or would be. Remember, everyone has competitors. You will need to gather as much information on your competitors as possible. You will need to spend some time on this activity, so don't rush through it. Take your time and do your research. All of this will help craft the marketing piece of your plan.

Market Research: The total size of your industry. Trends in the industry—is it growing or shrinking? What is the total size of your target market, and what share is realistic for you to obtain? Trends in the target market—is it growing or shrinking? How are customer needs or preferences changing?

_____

_____

_____

_____

_____

_____

_____

_____

_____

_____

_____

_____

_____

_____

_____

_____

_____

_____

_____

_____

_____

_____

_____

_____

_____

Target Market: Identify your target customer groups and create a demographic profile for each group that includes age, gender, location, income, occupation, education, and so on. The tighter your target market, the better.

_____

_____

_____

_____

_____

_____

_____

_____

_____

_____

_____

_____

_____

_____

_____

_____

_____

_____

_____

Key Competitors: List key companies that compete with you (including names and locations), as well as products that compete with yours and/or services that compete with yours. Do they compete across the board, or just for specific products, for certain customers, or in certain geographic areas? Also include indirect competitors. For instance, if you're opening a restaurant that relies on consumers' discretionary spending, then bars and nightclubs are indirect competitors.

Now, on to building your personal hashtag. For Entrepreneurship Empowered, I use that hashtag. But it is long, and when I am out guest speaking or presenting, I want to have people take pictures and tag me and my hashtag. So, I had to come up with something a little simpler. I also use EENMP as a hashtag. Those are my two primary business hashtags. I use them when I post. I also use other hashtags that relate to my industry, which is business and entrepreneurship. Right now, I want you to create some hashtags for your business and also think about what other hashtags you could use to connect to your product or service. Go to Instagram and Twitter and check out the hashtags. See if yours is being used. Then just search around in the hashtags for a while to see which ones have the most traffic. You will want a range of hashtags, and when you post, you will want to make sure to include them in your posting. You must be public in order for it to work and to draw in followers. When I create a grouping of hashtags—which, on Instagram, you can have a max of thirty—I place them in my notes on my phone. Most smartphones have a note section. I keep them there. Then, when I need them, I just copy and paste. Boom! All set and ready to go. On the space provided, create and build your hashtags. You may also write whatever you find as you are researching.

Chapter 6: *Financial Planning, Accounting, and Funding Your Business*

"If you don't take care of your money your money won't take care of you."

—**Mac Duke** in *The Strategist*

Know your numbers. You must know your numbers. So many businesses fail because the owners don't know their numbers. If you have never taken an accounting class, I suggest you do it. Even a managerial accounting class will serve you well. Chapter Six is full of valuable information and is a great place to start, but again, I want you to make sure you learn all you can about accounting and financial planning. There is no fear in understanding numbers. Yes, they can be complex, and it is a language of its own, but I need for you to learn the language and become EMPOWERED. The activities in this chapter are designed to help you put into practice accounting principles; gain a better understanding of the revenue model; research and calculate start-up costs; understand and create price strategies; understand and calculate your break-even point; explore and research the crowdfunding model; and get ahold of your own personal money with your third Entrepreneurship Empowered Challenge. If you are in my class, this is the one challenge you will be required to do. If you are not in my class, but you are in pursuit of taking the rights back to your life, then I suggest you also do this challenge and all of the challenges in this workbook.

Chapter 6, Activity 1: Accounting: Balance Sheet, Cost of Goods Sold, and Income Statement

The **balance sheet** is a financial report that shows what the company owes and what it owns, including shareholders' stake, at a point in time. The balance sheet has a formula that must be balanced. This is the fundamental accounting equation: Assets = Liabilities + Owner Equity. In Chapter Six of *Entrepreneurship Empowered*, there is an example of an already done balance sheet. You will also want to review the terms and definitions that are found in Chapter Six, as they will help you have a better understanding of the information provided below. The balance sheet provided below is for you to fill in the information. Give it a try and see how you do.

Accounts Receivable	$20,100
Land	$250,000
Notes Receivable	$10,200
Accounts Payable	$7,500
Common Stock	$316,000
Notes Payable (Long term)	$35,000
Retained Earnings	$243,300
Cash	$12,000
Notes Payable (Current)	$2,600
Buildings	$175,000
Equipment and Vehicles	$111,000
Goodwill	$15,000
Bonds Payable	$10,000
Ending Inventory	$21,100

Assets

Current Assets:

_____   _____

_____   _____

_____   _____

_____   _____

Total Current Assets: _____

Fixed Assets:

_____   _____

_____   _____

_____   _____

Total Fixed Assets: _____

Other Fixed Assets:

_____   _____

Total Other Fixed Assets: _____

Total Assets: ========================

Liabilities and Owners Equity

Current Liabilities:

_____   _____

_____   _____

Total Current Liabilities: _____

Long-Term Liabilities:

_____   _____

_____   _____

Total Long-Term Liabilities: _____

Owner Equity:

_____   _____

_____   _____

Total Owner Equity: _____

Total Liabilities and Owner Equity: ========================

Did it balance? Remember that it should balance, as this is a balance sheet. See the answer key in the back of the book.

Cost of Goods Sold is going to tell you how much you made from selling your goods. It is a simple math equation. The formula is as follows: Beginning inventory + purchases made = Cost of Goods Available for Sale − Ending Inventory = Cost of Goods Sold. That's it. You will see that the Cost of Goods Sold will appear in the income statement, which you will try next. For now, give the Cost of Goods Sold activity a try. (Answer key in the back.)

Calculate the Cost of Goods Sold if a business has:
     $14,000 cost of inventory at the beginning of the year
     $8,000 cost of additional inventory purchased during the year
     $10,000 ending inventory
Answer: _____

_____

_____

_____

_____

You own a T-shirt business. At the beginning of the month, you have a T-shirt inventory balance of $300.00. During the month, you purchase an additional 100 T-shirts for $1,000.00. Then you sell some T-shirts. Thus, your inventory balance at the end of the month is $800.00. Calculate the cost of goods available for sale and the cost of goods sold for the month.
Answer: _____

_____

_____

_____

A company starts the month with $10,000.00 of inventory on hand, expends $25,000.00 on various inventory items during the month, and has $8,000.00 of inventory on hand at the end of the month. What is the cost of goods sold during the month?

_____

_____

_____

_____

_____

_____

The **income statement** is a financial report that measures the financial performance of your business on a monthly or annual basis. The income statement tells you just that: how much income (profit) you made. I want you to always be in the black. Not in the red. If you haven't heard the saying *being in the black or red*, let me tell you what it means. The **black means profit**, and the **red means loss.** Some businesses do go into the red. It is common for startups to be in the red, but you don't want to stay there. You simply cannot stay there and survive in business. Again, in Chapter Six of *Entrepreneurship Empowered* is an example of a completed income statement. You may look there to help you do the following activity. The terms and definitions will also be helpful to you.

Use the following data to complete the income statement:

Insurance Expenses	$9,000
Interest Expenses	$4,100
Net Sales	$175,500
Ending Inventory	$21,100
Beginning Inventory	$25,800
Advertising Expense	$15,000
Salaries	$30,000
Merchandise Purchased	$52,800
Rent	$2,300
Utilities	$1,400

Revenue/Net Sales: _____

Cost of Goods Sold: _____

  Beginning Inventory: _____

+ Merchandise Purchased: _____

Cost of Goods Available for Sale:_____

 · Ending Inventory: _____

Cost of Goods Sold: _____

Gross Profit: _____

Operating Expenses:

_____ _____

_____ _____

_____ _____

_____ _____

_____ _____

_____ _____

Total Operating Expenses: _____

Net Income Before Taxes: _____

 ·income taxes (33%): _____

Net Income After Taxes: _____

How did you do? The answer key is in the back of the book.

Chapter 6, Activity 2: Revenue Model

Revenue is defined in accounting as "*the income that a business has from its normal business activities, usually from the sale of goods and services to customers. Revenue is also referred to as sales or turnover. Some companies receive revenue from interest, royalties, or other fees.*" In *Entrepreneurship Empowered*, you must understand the revenue model, which is a framework for how you will generate income for your business. You must have a revenue strategy. You will want to start by asking yourself some questions:

How much are my customers willing to pay? (This will require some research to find out what customers are willing to pay.)

_____

_____

_____

_____

_____

_____

_____

_____

_____

_____

_____

_____

How many customers do I need?

_____

_____

_____

_____

_____

_____

_____

_____

_____

_____

_____

How much revenue can be generated through sales?

_____
_____
_____
_____
_____
_____
_____
_____
_____
_____
_____
_____
_____

If I have more than one revenue stream, how much does each stream contribute to the total?

_____
_____
_____
_____
_____
_____
_____
_____
_____
_____
_____

Chapter 6, Activity 3: Start-Up Costs

For this activity, you will once again need to do some research. Remember that there is no one-size-fits-all for businesses, especially with start-up costs. Each business is going to have its own set of start-up and operational costs. The following are common start-up costs you are likely to have, no matter what business type:

- Office space
- Equipment and supplies
- Communications
- Utilities
- Licenses and permits
- Insurance
- Inventory
- Employee salaries
- Advertising and marketing
- Market research
- Printed marketing material
- Making a website
- Lawyers and accountants

Don't underestimate your start-up costs. Do your research! I would even encourage you to add 5–10% to each of your start-up costs. Using the space provided, write all the start-up and operational costs you come up with. This information will help you with how you should price your product and what your break-even point is. (Those are the next two activities.)

_____

_____

_____

_____

_____

_____

_____

_____

_____

_____

_____

_____

_____

_____

_____

Chapter 6, Activity 4: Pricing Strategies

There are several ways to price your products. Read over the different ways you can price your product. Then, on the space provided, write what you think you will charge for your products or services.

Competition-led pricing is where prices match those of your competitors. Understand that just because you have the same price as your competitor doesn't mean a customer will buy from you. You will need to differentiate your business.

Customer-led pricing is what the customer is willing to pay. You will need to ask your target market what they think the price should be. Priceline is known for this, as they allow customers to bid on the price. They do, of course, have the power to accept or reject the price. But again, the customer is leading the price.

Loss-leader pricing sets the price below cost. This strategy is used to attract more customers. Special discounts or reducing of a price is offered in this type of strategy.

Introductory offer is a strategy where people are offered free or heavily discounted pricing to try a new product. It could be even something like the first 50 customers receive the product for 75% off.

Price skimming is when a business sets the highest initial price on a product, then lowers it over time. This is commonly used for new products or services that have very little or no competition. Bigger known innovation companies use this strategy often.

Psychological pricing is used all the time, and the consumer eats it up. To the consumer mind, anything ending in either .99 or .95 is more appealing because it gives consumers the illusion that they're saving money. Flash sales such as buy one, get one free are also ways to use the psychological pricing strategy.

Now that you have some of the most common pricing strategies, use the space provided to figure out how you are going to set your prices. Remember to reflect on your costs that are involved, both fixed and variable costs.

_____

_____

_____

_____

_____

_____

_____

_____

_____

_____

_____

Chapter 6, Activity 5: Break-Even Point

It is very important that you understand what your break-even point is. You are going to need to know what all your fixed and variable costs are. Below is an example of how to figure out your break-even point. Review the example and then work on giving it a try.

Entrepreneurship Empowered has calculated that it has fixed costs that consist of its rent, depreciation of its assets, salaries, and taxes. Those fixed costs add up to $60,000. Their product is a star bookmarker. Their variable costs associated with producing the product is raw material, labor, and commissions. Variable costs have been calculated to be $0.80 per unit. The product is priced at $2.00 each. Given this information, we can calculate the break-even point for the product, using the following formula: Fixed cost divided by price of product minus variable cost equals number of units needed to sale to break even.

$60,000 ÷ ($2.00 - $0.80) = 50,000 units

Using the formula for the example given, Entrepreneurship Empowered would need to sell $50,000 bookmarkers to break even. Now, if they raise the price of the bookmark from $2.00 to $3.95, the number of units to sell would change.

$60,000 ÷ ($3.95 - $0.80) = 19,048 units

With the price change, they don't need to sell as many. They now break even at 19,048 units sold. Let's say raising the price is not the better solution. They may then look for a way to cut costs. First, they look at their fixed cost and see right away they can reduce their fixed cost by $10,000. Now let's see what the new break-even point would be.

$50,000 ÷ ($2.00-$0.80) = 41,666 units

See how you can play with the numbers to figure out which is the better solution? Remember to always look for efficiency in the way you spend your money. This is why you were given the task to track your money. The better you are with your personal money, the better you will be with the money of your business.

Breaking even is a good thing as long as you have included all costs in the calculations. Many times, entrepreneurs forget to pay themselves. They don't even indicate what their salary should be. They just say, "I'll pay myself later because right now, I don't have the money to pay myself." This may be true, but you still need to allocate your salary. Remember to include that in your calculation. Use the space provided to work on your break-even point.

Chapter 6, Activity 6: Crowdfunding

There are many different crowdfunding sites in the market today. I would like for you to do a little research on the following top four. Make notes as you research, using the space provided. You should be able to find pros and cons, as well as important information like how much of a cut they take from what you raise, and whether there are any additional charges. The research you gather will help you to select which site is best for your business needs. The top four sites are *Kickstarter, GoFundMe, Indiegogo, and Patreon.*

Entrepreneurship Empowered Challenge Three: Money Tracking Challenge

If you are not able to handle your own money, how in the hell do you think you will be able to handle a business's money? Businesses fail time and time again from being poorly managed. There are people in business today who are making money, but they don't know how to keep money. They are borrowing money to make payroll. How is that? Why is that? They don't know how to keep money because they have poor spending habits and they mismanage money. This third challenge is going to show you how to manage your own money. You will track your money for two weeks. If you can track longer, I highly recommend it. The longer you track, the more you will learn about your spending habits. Make sure when you track that you write down everything you spent—to the penny. Make sure to total each day what you spent and then total what you spent over the course of the two weeks. After you finish tracking, I need you to examine your findings carefully. Do you handle your money well? Could you do better? Was there a surprise along the way? What did you learn from the experience? You are going to write about the experience and all you learned. Then, you will work on setting goals to manage your money better. Even if you do manage your money well—can you do better? If so, how will you do better? Are you ready to be EMPOWERED? Then get to tracking!

Date	Day of the week	Item(s) Purchased	Amount

Date	Day of the week	Item(s) Purchased	Amount

Date	Day of the week	Item(s) Purchased	Amount

Now that your tracking time has come to a close, I want you to reflect and examine how you spend your money. How well do you spend money? Did you have things coming out of your account that you didn't know about? Such as a subscription that you don't use? Do you eat out every day, and is it adding up? Do you have a habit that is consuming a nice chunk of your money? What did you discover from tracking your money? What did you learn? Reflect on everything and then create some money goals and some savings goals. Make a plan on how you will manage your money better. How are you going to be EMPOWERED with the way you handle your money?

_____

_____

_____

_____

_____

_____

_____

_____

_____

Chapter 7: *Leadership and Ethics*

"Before you are a leader, success is all about growing yourself. When you become a leader, success is all about growing others."

—Jack Welch, former CEO of General Electric

Leadership and ethics are mission-critical to *Entrepreneurship Empowered*. There are two leadership theories I write about in my book—Situational Leadership and Transformation Leadership. I believe in both theories, and they are certainly part of my leadership style. Empowered Leadership is about creating more leaders, not more followers. But in leadership, what you have are people who follow you. You should be empowering them at all levels. Please keep in mind that only things are to be managed. People are to be led. Leading by example is a perfect place to start. Being an ethical person and doing what is right, even when no one is watching, is extremely important.

You will need your book for this next activity so you can see the Situational and Transformation Leadership charts. After you work on those activities, you will move on to a leadership survey to see where you fall with your leadership skills. After that, you will close the chapter by analyzing an ethical dilemma case. You will certainly want to have your book open and available to use for the activities in this chapter.

Chapter 7, Activity 1: Situational Leadership

Below is a set of situations. You are going to choose what to do, and what you choose to do will indicate what type of leadership style you used. Go to Chapter Seven in *Entrepreneurship Empowered* and use the charts to help you.

1. You are the project manager of a six-man team. You encourage your team and notice that they work well together. However, a conflict arises between two team members regarding which idea to use in the next stage of the project. As their leader, you: _____

_____

_____

_____

_____

_____

_____

_____

What is your leadership style? _____

_____

2. You are the new head basketball coach. You notice that morale is low, the players are not performing at the level you know they are capable of, and they lack new skill techniques that you know will help them be more successful in the game. In a meeting, you: _____

_____

_____

_____

_____

_____

_____

What is your leadership style? _____

_____

3. You hire a new employee who has a strong administrative skill set. After only a few weeks with the new employee, you can tell she is innovative and communicates well with clients. At first, you: _____

_____

_____

_____

_____

_____

_____

What is your leadership style? _____

4. You ask one of your long-time employees to take on a new task. His past performance shows that he has done well with your direction and support. The new task is important in making sure the project is completed on time. He may not have all the skills needed to do the task, but he is enthusiastic about the new challenge. You: _____

_____

_____

_____

_____

What is your leadership style? _____

_____

5. Your organization has recently seen an increase in work. You have asked one of your employees to take on a new responsibility. You have worked with him for several years now, and you know that he has the knowledge and skills to be successful. However, he seems insecure about his ability to do the job. You decide to: _____

_____

_____

_____

_____

_____

_____

_____

What is your leadership style? _____

_____

6. You are the dean in the business department of a college that is doing well. Student success is important to you. You would like student retention to increase, and you would also like to increase graduation rates. You decide to: _____

_____

_____

_____

_____

_____

_____

_____

What is your leadership style? _____

_____

Chapter 7, Activity 2: Transformational Leadership

Again, you will need your book to read over what transformation leadership theory is. It is, however, straightforward and based on motivation. So, for this activity, I want you to think about ways you will be able to motivate staff as a leader. How are you going to motivate them? How are you going to set goals and put rewards in place? What do you believe will be important for everyone on the team to understand, and how are you going to convey that message as their leader? Just take some time to think and write what comes to you.

_____

_____

_____

_____

_____

_____

_____

_____

_____

_____

_____

_____

_____

_____

_____

_____

_____

_____

_____

_____

_____

_____

Chapter 7, Activity 3: Self-Analysis Leadership Survey

The following is a self-assessment for you to take. Remember to be honest, as this is for you only. You will circle the answer and total the points at the end. Then, with the score, you will see there is a rubric that will indicate what your leadership level is.

1. I am an effective communicator and enjoy speaking to people.
   a.   Almost Always True — 5
   b.   Frequently True — 4
   c.   Occasionally True — 3
   d.   Seldom True — 2
   e.   Almost Never True — 1

2. I have integrity and a strong moral compass. I believe in doing what is right.
   a.   Almost Always True — 5
   b.   Frequently True — 4
   c.   Occasionally True — 3
   d.   Seldom True — 2
   e.   Almost Never True — 1

3. I am open to making decisions with other inputs.
   a.   Almost Always True — 5
   b.   Frequently True — 4
   c.   Occasionally True — 3
   d.   Seldom True — 2
   e.   Almost Never True — 1

4. My behaviors and actions are consistent. I can be counted on.
   a.   Almost Always True — 5
   b.   Frequently True — 4
   c.   Occasionally True — 3
   d.   Seldom True — 2
   e.   Almost Never True — 1

5. I do well at delegating and am able to give people instructions on what they need to do.
   a.   Almost Always True — 5
   b.   Frequently True — 4
   c.   Occasionally True — 3
   d.   Seldom True — 2
   e.   Almost Never True — 1

6. I am an effective listener, am open to feedback, and I ask questions.
   a.   Almost Always True — 5
   b.   Frequently True — 4
   c.   Occasionally True — 3
   d.   Seldom True — 2
   e.   Almost Never True — 1

7. I follow up as a way to keep focus.
   a.   Almost Always True — 5
   b.   Frequently True — 4

     c.   Occasionally True — 3

     d.   Seldom True — 2

     e.   Almost Never True — 1

8. I am a very loyal person to those I serve.

     a.   Almost Always True — 5

     b.   Frequently True — 4

     c.   Occasionally True — 3

     d.   Seldom True — 2

     e.   Almost Never True — 1

9. I believe in growth and the growth mindset.

     a.   Almost Always True — 5

     b.   Frequently True — 4

     c.   Occasionally True — 3

     d.   Seldom True — 2

     e.   Almost Never True — 1

10. I have a big vision and see widely.

     a.   Almost Always True — 5

     b.   Frequently True — 4

     c.   Occasionally True — 3

     d.   Seldom True — 2

     e.   Almost Never True — 1

11. I offer praise and acknowledge good and great work.

     a.   Almost Always True — 5

     b.   Frequently True — 4

     c.   Occasionally True — 3

     d.   Seldom True — 2

     e.   Almost Never True — 1

12. I am able to give constructive criticism and address issues quickly.

     a.   Almost Always True — 5

     b.   Frequently True — 4

     c.   Occasionally True — 3

     d.   Seldom True — 2

     e.   Almost Never True — 1

13. Plan developing is a core strength of mine.

     a.   Almost Always True — 5

     b.   Frequently True — 4

     c.   Occasionally True — 3

     d.   Seldom True — 2

     e.   Almost Never True — 1

14. I set goals, objectives, and I can see the vision of where I am going.

     a.   Almost Always True — 5

     b.   Frequently True — 4

     c.   Occasionally True — 3

     d.   Seldom True — 2

     e.   Almost Never True — 1

15. I am resilient and flexible.

     a.   Almost Always True — 5

    b.   Frequently True — 4

    c.   Occasionally True — 3

    d.   Seldom True — 2

    e.   Almost Never True — 1

16. I am available and have an open door policy with those I work with and for.

    a.   Almost Always True — 5

    b.   Frequently True — 4

    c.   Occasionally True — 3

    d.   Seldom True — 2

    e.   Almost Never True — 1

17. I am a self-starter and a take-charge type of person.

    a.   Almost Always True — 5

    b.   Frequently True — 4

    c.   Occasionally True — 3

    d.   Seldom True — 2

    e.   Almost Never True — 1

18. I am calm under pressure.

    a.   Almost Always True — 5

    b.   Frequently True — 4

    c.   Occasionally True — 3

    d.   Seldom True — 2

    e.   Almost Never True — 1

19. I am able to set boundaries and keep a team in line.

    a.   Almost Always True — 5

    b.   Frequently True — 4

    c.   Occasionally True — 3

    d.   Seldom True — 2

    e.   Almost Never True — 1

20. I am good at coaching and being supportive.

    a.   Almost Always True — 5

    b.   Frequently True — 4

    c.   Occasionally True — 3

    d.   Seldom True — 2

    e.   Almost Never True — 1

21. I know how to sell.

    a.   Almost Always True — 5

    b.   Frequently True — 4

    c.   Occasionally True — 3

    d.   Seldom True — 2

    e.   Almost Never True — 1

22. I am curious.

    a.   Almost Always True — 5

    b.   Frequently True — 4

    c.   Occasionally True — 3

    d.   Seldom True — 2

    e.   Almost Never True — 1

23. I have emotional intelligence and can see what is really going on with others.
   a.   Almost Always True — 5
   b.   Frequently True — 4
   c.   Occasionally True — 3
   d.   Seldom True — 2
   e.   Almost Never True — 1
24. I understand there is power in people.
   a.   Almost Always True — 5
   b.   Frequently True — 4
   c.   Occasionally True — 3
   d.   Seldom True — 2
   e.   Almost Never True — 1
25. I am not afraid to be transparent.
   a.   Almost Always True — 5
   b.   Frequently True — 4
   c.   Occasionally True — 3
   d.   Seldom True — 2
   e.   Almost Never True — 1

What is your score?_____. The maximum score is 125, and the minimum score is 25.

- 87 and above: You are well on your way to becoming a leader.
- 63 to 86: You are getting close.
- 62 and below: Don't Give Up! Many before you have continued with their studies to become some of the finest leaders around. You, too, can grow into an EMPOWERED Leader if you just keep training.

Chapter 7, Activity 4: Ethical Dilemma Case Study

At some point in our lives, we will all come across many different ethical dilemmas, and I encourage you to always choose the best solution. However, an ethical dilemma is sometimes like choosing between two evils. So, what do you do then? Below is an ethical case dilemma that I want you to read over and then decide what you are going to do. I want you to think about all the people involved. Who are the innocent bystanders? Based on the decision you make, how will those people be affected? Really dig deep into thought and use your moral compass to direct your decisions.

Ethical Dilemma:

Imagine you are the owner of a large company. You have very loyal and longstanding clients and employees. You are known for being an ethically sound company, and your social responsibility is secure. Your top manager has been with you for over twenty years. You have been the main support for this employee and his/her family for all twenty years. You have their seen children grow from little ones to college students. They are at every holiday party and, truth be told, you couldn't have built your business without this top manager. You just received word that the production of your highest profit-generating product, which is produced in another country, is using child labor. You really don't want to find out more because you already hear about the harsh labor conditions, and these are young children. But you must make a decision. In order to stop using child labor, you must fire your top manager. Do you keep the top manager and keep using child labor? Are there any other solutions? Take some time to think about this dilemma and write all that comes to you. Make a decision and give the reasoning why you made this decision.

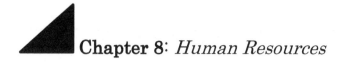

Chapter 8: *Human Resources*

"I am convinced that nothing we do is more important than hiring and developing people. At the end of the day, you bet on people not on strategies."

—Lawrence Bossidy, former CEO of AlliedSignal

There are many books written on how to manage human resources. The following activities will help you as you begin to think about having employees. Remember, we are in the human economy—a very powerful economy. Human capital is very beneficial to your business. You will need to ensure you take good care of your employees. You will want to hire and retain the best of the best. You are to never hold on too tightly to them, because, remember, a true leader builds up more leaders, not more followers. That being said, you will have loyal employees who will be with you for many years, if not the entire time you are in business. We are going to start brainstorming what might be the top 21st Century Soft Skills needed. Then you are going to figure out what you will want to have in your new hire paperwork and an outline for an employee handbook. Lastly, you will close out this chapter by creating an onboarding process for your employees.

Chapter 8, Activity 1: Top 21st Century Soft Skills

I want you to think for a moment or two about what you think would be the most important 21st Century Soft Skills an employee would need to have. Think about it from the perspective of the business you are building. Think about it from what you have experienced already in the workforce. Then, in the space provided, I want you to list all that comes to mind. You may look in the book to see what I have indicated as the top 21st Century Soft Skills according to the New World of Work (NWoW). However, for your business, I want you to list out what you believe are the most important. This is what you will be looking for when you begin to hire employees.

_____

_____

_____

_____

_____

_____

_____

_____

_____

Chapter 8, Activity 2: Creating a New Hire Packet and Employee Handbook

You will want to use your book for this section, and you can also do a Google search. I want you to indicate what will need to be in your new hire paperwork. I want you to describe how you will process the paperwork, how you plan to file it, how you will keep it organized, and so on. Then, I want you to spend some time thinking about what you will need to include in a new employee handbook. What do you believe is going to be important information that will help each of your employees? Remember, when putting your paperwork together, you think about non-competition and or intellectual property protection with any trade secrets and the like. Again, be a researcher and see what is already out there. Then, then using the space provided, write out your plan.

Chapter 8, Activity 3: Creating an Onboarding Process

It always surprises me to find out how many businesses do not have an onboarding process. This is not going to be the case with your business because you are an EMPOWERED ENTREPRENEUR. If you train your employees right the first time, you don't have to train them over and over again. So, make sure to start off with a solid onboarding process. I want you to spend some time thinking about all the steps that are needed to be covered in training. Don't leave anything out. No matter how skilled someone is, they will still need to know how you like the business to be run, how you like things to be done, and how your specific system works. Just spend some time thinking and draft what you believe would be a start to an onboarding process. This is just to get you thinking because, unless you are already in business, you cannot know for certain that what you come up with will work. And remember, each employee will learn and train differently. It would be wise to have them take a VARK survey to find out what their learning style is. VARK is an acronym for Visual, Aural, Read/Write, and Kinesthetic. Once you know what their most dominant learning style is, then you can teach them in that style. I do suggest you do some research about onboarding and see what you come up with. Use the space provided to write what you find.

# Chapter 9: *Launch, Manage, and Grow*

"Your work is going to fill a large part of your life, and the only way to be truly satisfied is to do what you believe is great work. And the only way to do great work is to love what you do."

—Steve Jobs, co-founder, former chairman and CEO of Apple

Chapter Nine is a big chapter, and I highly recommend you read it over several times to fully digest the information found within. The next set of activities will be extremely helpful as you begin to set up your business and launch it. First, you will need to do some research. You may even want to go meet with your local business centers, insurance agents, and visit SCORE (www.score.org) or SBA (see below) for information. We are going to start with some step-by-step processes, then move on to an insurance and bank account search, and I will close out on helping you understand your taxes. Please keep in mind that it is always wise to seek legal counsel and to work directly with an accountant to help advise you on exactly what to do. This is a general overview of the steps and preliminary research for your greater knowledge.

Chapter 9, Activity 1: Step-By-Step Process on How to File for a Doing Business as (DBA), Employer Identification Number (EIN), and a Dun & Bradstreet Number (DUNS)

If you are going to do business under any name other than your legal name, you will want to do a DBA. If you want to open a business bank account, which you do, you must have a DBA. Each county differs in how you apply for a DBA, so the first thing you will want to do is contact your county clerk or recorder's office and ask them what the filing process is for a DBA. I am going to give you some general steps, but then I am providing you with space to write what you find from doing your research.

1. Name search is done via the county clerk's or recorder's office. You will need to ensure no one else is using the name you have selected as your DBA. Of course, if it is taken, then you will need to select another name. With your name, please keep in mind that in California you will need to ensure you don't use Incorporated (Inc.), Corporation (Corp), or Limited Liability Corporation (LLC) if the business is not legally formed as one of those business structures in either California or another jurisdiction.
2. File appropriate paperwork with the county clerk or recorder's office and pay a filing fee.
3. Publish in a local paper that you are doing business as the name you have filed. This is required and must be done within 30 days of filing.

Those are the basic steps. Space has been provided for you to write what you find from your local county clerk's or recorder's office. Remember, a quick Google search will locate the contact information of the county office you need to contact.

If you plan to have employees, you are required by law to have an EIN. It is a very simple process. The following steps are how you file for and obtain an EIN. The following information comes directly off the IRS website[10] (see below). As I have stated before, I highly suggest you explore both the SBA and IRS websites as they will be one of your top resources in business.

1. "Determine Eligibility: You may apply for an EIN online if your principal business is located in the United States or U.S. Territories. The person applying online must have a valid Taxpayer Identification Number (SSN, ITIN, EIN). You are limited to one EIN per responsible party per day. The 'responsible party' is the person who ultimately owns or controls the entity or who exercises ultimate effective control over the entity. Unless the applicant is a government entity, the responsible party must be an individual (i.e., a natural person), not an entity."

2. Understand the Online Application: "You must complete this application in one session, as you will not be able to save and return at a later time. Your session will expire after 15 minutes of inactivity, and you will need to start over."

3. Submit Your Application: "After all validations are done, you will get your EIN immediately upon completion. You can then download, save, and print your EIN confirmation notice."

You see how simple that is. Now go to www.irs.gov and search for EIN and then read all that you find. Make notes in the space provided. I suggest you even click on the apply button and take a look at what the application looks like. Remember that the more knowledge you have, the more EMPOWERED you are!

_____

_____

_____

_____

_____

_____

_____

_____

_____

_____

_____

_____

_____

_____

_____

_____

A DUNS number is yet another number you will want to acquire when doing business. It is also a very simple process. DUNS stands for Data Universal Numbering System. Dun & Bradstreet are the developers and controllers of the DUNS number. It is a unique number for your business. It is used for business credit. If you plan to bid on any government proposals, you must have a DUNS number. When registering for your DUNS number, you'll need to have the following on hand:

- Legal name
- Headquarters name and address for your business
- Doing Business As (DBA) or other name by which your business is commonly recognized
- Physical address, city, state, and ZIP Code
- Mailing address (if different from headquarters and/or physical address)
- Telephone number
- Contact name and title
- Number of employees at your physical location
- Whether you're a home-based business

Now I would like for you to go to Dun & Bradstreet's website[11] and explore. Then write down what you found in your research. Take notes. You may not wish to file for a DUNS number now, but you are collecting information to ensure you are ready when the time comes. www.dnb.com.

_____

_____

_____

_____

_____

_____

_____

_____

_____

_____

_____

_____

_____

_____

_____

_____

Chapter 9, Activity 2: Insurance Search

Now we are going to turn our attention to insurance. The following information comes directly from the SBA's website.[12]

- **General liability insurance**: Any business. This coverage protects against financial loss as the result of bodily injury, property damage, medical expenses, libel, slander, defending lawsuits, and settlement bonds or judgments.
- **Product liability insurance**: Businesses that manufacture, wholesale, distribute, and retail a product. This coverage protects against financial loss as a result of a defective product that causes injury or bodily harm.
- **Professional liability insurance**: Businesses that provide services to customers. This coverage protects against financial loss as a result of malpractice, errors, and negligence.
- **Commercial property insurance**: Businesses with a significant amount of property and physical assets. This coverage protects your business against loss and damage of company property due to a wide variety of events such as fire, smoke, wind, and hail storms, civil disobedience, and vandalism.
- **Home-based business insurance**: Businesses that are run out of the owner's personal home. Coverage that's added to homeowner's insurance as a rider can offer protection for a small amount of business equipment and liability coverage for third-party injuries.
- **Business owner's policy**: Most small business owners, but especially home-based business owners. A business owner's policy is an insurance package that combines all of the typical coverage options into one bundle. They simplify the insurance-buying process and can save you money.

Four steps to buy business insurance:

1. Assess your risks. Think about what kind of accidents, natural disasters, or lawsuits could damage your business. If you need help, the National Federation of Independent Businesses (NFIB) provides information for choosing insurance to help you assess your risks and to make sure you've insured every aspect of your business.
2. Find a reputable licensed agent. Commercial insurance agents can help you find policies that match your business needs. They receive commissions from insurance companies when they sell policies, so it's important to find a licensed agent that's interested in your needs as much as his/her own.
3. Shop around. Prices and benefits can vary significantly. You should compare rates, terms, and benefits for insurance offers from several different agents.
4. Reassess every year. As your business grows, so do your liabilities. If you have purchased or replaced equipment or expanded operations, you should contact your insurance agent to discuss changes in your business and how they affect your coverage.

Now I want you to call around or do a Google search for insurance. You can look for most commonly needed or used insurance for your industry. I want you to find out what the policy covers, how much is the deductible, what is the cost of the insurance, and then ask any other questions you can think of. In the space provided, write what you find from your research.

Chapter 9, Activity 3: Business Bank Account

You are going to need a business bank account. It is very important to keep your personal and business funds separate. Only use the business account for business. Don't mingle them together. That is bad for business. Once you have your DBA, you can take that to the bank and open a business bank account. You will also want to make sure to develop a professional business relationship with your banker. You will find in business that building relationships is mission-critical to the success of your business. You are now going to research banks and find out all you can regarding the business accounts at each bank. Remember, the more you find out, the better. Knowledge is power. In the space provided, write all that you find from your research.

Chapter 9, Activity 4: Understanding Your Taxes

"Death and taxes are two sure things in life." That is the saying, right? Well, in business, you must understand your taxes. The following information comes directly from the SBA,[12] and after you understand the information, I want you to spend a little time thinking about how you are going to handle taxes. I also want you to write yourself a promise that if you ever have trouble with your taxes, you will find some help or call the IRS with no fear. I can promise you they are there to help you. You cannot run from them.

Choose your tax year

Your business is legally required to pay taxes and keep accounting records on a consistent yearly schedule called a tax year.

Most businesses choose their tax year to be the same as the calendar year. You select your tax year the first time you file for taxes, but you can change it later with permission from the IRS.

Calendar tax year if you don't have special accounting needs for your business.

Fiscal tax year if you want your 12-month accounting cycle to end in a month that isn't December.

Short tax year if your business wasn't in existence for an entire tax year, or you changed your accounting period.

If your business doesn't have much reporting or bookkeeping, you might be required to use a calendar tax year. Check with the IRS for detailed rules about tax years.

Determine your state tax obligations

Your business might need to pay state and local taxes. Tax laws vary by location and business structure, so you'll need to check with state and local governments to know your business's tax obligations.

The two most common types of state and local tax requirements for small business are income taxes and employment taxes.

Your state income tax obligations are determined by your business structure. For example, corporations are taxed separately from the owners, while sole proprietors report their personal and business income taxes using the same form.

If your business has employees, you'll be responsible for paying state employment taxes. These vary by state but often include workers' compensation insurance, unemployment insurance taxes, and temporary disability insurance. You might also be responsible for withholding employee income tax. Check with your state tax authority to find out how much you need to withhold and when you need to send it to the state.

Determine your federal tax obligations

Your business structure determines what federal taxes you must pay and how you pay them. Some of the taxes require payment throughout the year, so it's important to know your tax obligations before the end of your tax year.

There are five general types of business taxes:
1. Income tax

2. Self-employment tax
3. Estimated tax
4. Employer tax
5. Excise tax

Each category of business tax might have special rules, qualifications, or IRS forms you need to file. Check with the IRS to see which business taxes apply to you.

If your business has employees, you might be required to withhold taxes from their paychecks. Federal employment taxes include income, Social Security and Medicare, unemployment, and self-employment taxes. Check with the IRS to see which taxes you need to withhold.

Now go take a look at the IRS website and explore the tax links. Then make a note of what you find and also include how you plan to handle your taxes. Don't forget to write your promise to yourself. The way out is within.

 **Chapter 10**: *The 10 Core Palumbo Principles*

"You can, you should, and if you're brave enough to start, you will."

—Stephen King, *On Writing: A Memoir of the Craft*

The 10 core Palumbo Principles are ones I believe will help you live the EMPOWERED LIFE. In this chapter, you will find your final activities and final Entrepreneurship Empowered challenge. I can only imagine how much you have grown and developed. I can promise you that all of the activities and challenges in this workbook have been designed not only to make you stronger in business and in life, but they have been designed to EMPOWER you. For this first activity, you are going to write your empowerment statement. I am providing my example. I have always been a people-pleaser, and that is one area in which I have chosen to be EMPOWERED. You, too, may be a people-pleaser. If that's where you need to be EMPOWERED, then start there. Many times, students will say, "I don't want to take what you have, but I have the same issue. May I write about it?" Absolutely! This is why I share my story so openly and publicly, because I know that I am not alone, and I am here to inspire. I am here to EMPOWER you. The dictionary defines "empower" **as: make (someone) stronger and more confident, especially in controlling their life and claiming their rights.** In the space provided, you are going to write your personal empowerment statement. This will help you unlock the key to opening the door to living the EMPOWERED LIFE. Remember that the way out is within.

Chapter 10, Activity 1: Empowerment Statement
Empowered Statement—My Example:

I am a people-pleaser, and many times have become so hurt by family, friends, and people in general. What I am learning is that it is unhealthy to be a people-pleaser. It can actually make you sick and has many times made me sick. The side effects of abuse are nothing nice. Being a people-pleaser is one of my side effects. But I am healing and will continue to heal and be free. I have decided to be EMPOWERED and no longer subject myself to people-pleasing. I will choose to say "NO!" and have no remorse. I will say "YES" to me! I am confident in myself and the purpose of my life. I know that I am not able to please everyone, nor will I inspire everyone, but I have had visions where I have seen seas upon seas of people who will be inspired by my life story. I will be used to give hope to so many that feel hopeless. I will be used to help heal and set others free. This pleases me.

Now it is your turn. In what area do you need to be more EMPOWERED?

_____

_____

_____

Chapter 10, Activity 2: BVIG's and Empowered Life Goal Setting

My very good friend and personal trainer, Cesar Figueroa, turned me on to the BVIG's. "B" stands for belief. What do you believe in? "V" stands for values. What are your top values? "I" stands for intentions. What is it that you are looking to embody? "G" stands for gratitude. What are you grateful for?

For this activity, you are going to write out what your BVIG's are, and then you are going to set your EMPOWERED LIFE goals. A 3-month, a 6-month, and a 1-year goal. Remember, you are designed to live the EMPOWERED LIFE. This is what it takes—living your BVIG's daily. Using the space provided, I want you to write out your BVIG's and goals. For "belief," I want you to put your beliefs in a statement. I am healthy. I am well. I am beautiful. I am healed. I am free. I am a life-changer. I am amazing. I am EMPOWERED, and so on. Whatever your positive beliefs are, write them out. Then, for your values, I want you to list your top 10 values. Then circle your top 5 out of those 10. Then from those 5, I want you to highlight your top 3. Out of those 3, what is number 1? Rewrite that one word in very large print and doodle around it or color it or do something to make it stand out. That is your core value. The one that you value the very most. That value should be leading your life. When you make decisions in life, you need to ask yourself if they match up with your top 3 values.

I truly believe in being less habitual and more intentional. So again, for intention, you are asking yourself what do you wish to embody and/or create? Remember that as Empowered Entrepreneurs, we don't predict our future; we create it. And as Empowered individuals, we do the same. Write out your intentions: new behaviors that will lead to new ways of thinking. Change your mind, and you change your future. Be clear on what you create but release any and all time expectations. The vision will appear if you faint not. It is always on time. Most importantly, I need you to walk daily in a spirit of gratitude. You see, gratitude, joy, appreciation, love, and bliss all have a high frequency. By giving gratitude for our beliefs, values, and intentions, we are activating our higher frequency and pulling those things to us. When we are at a higher frequency, we are open to how intentions will manifest. High energy has high power. Our thoughts are powerful. Our words give command over our lives. There is power of life and death in the tongue. So, each morning I want you to speak out loud your BVIG's. In the morning, when you wake up, give your gratitude—starting with your beliefs. Say them out loud. Then move on to your top values. Give gratitude for being a person of value and being true to your core values. Then read out loud your intentions and—this is a very important step—RELEASE them! Remember, they will return to you in the time they are called to. You are to keep the faith. Feel the joy and walk forward in the bliss. Activate those frequencies and be thankful for receiving what you desire. Then you are open to receive what the day holds for you. This is living the EMPOWERED LIFE because the way out is within.

Now it is time to write. Start with your BVIG's, then do your EMPOWERED LIFE goals. And remember to speak your truth every day.

Entrepreneurship Empowered Challenge Four: Legacy Letter

Writing a legacy letter is one of the hardest things I have ever done. While earning my master's degree, a professor gave us the assignment to write a legacy letter. I had never heard of such a thing. I can clearly see myself weeping like a baby at my desk as I wrote my son a final goodbye. You see, that is what a legacy letter is. It is a letter from you to your legacy—to your family and friends. You project yourself to your death bed and you write. It can take a toll on your emotions because, no matter how strong your faith is, the sting of death is very real. But we all will cross over one day. I am a true believer that love is the only thing that is real, everything—and I mean everything—else is an illusion. Love never dies, but it does transcend—as each of us will do one day. I believe we have been given one commission here on earth, and that is to love. And we screw it up every day and three times on Sunday. This is why I share my message. This why I live out loud. This is why the EMPOWERED series is within me. It is in my writings that I get to live, and the same is true for you. So, I encourage you to write. This one challenge is not a required one, but a suggested one. I understand that doing this challenge is very difficult, and many are not ready. But I desire to see you live the EMPOWERED LIFE. This is why I give you key after key to help set you free. As I have stated time and time again, the way out is within. Though this challenge is hard and difficult, I encourage you to write the letter. Go to your death bed, what type of life did you live? What do you want to say to your children and loved ones? What do you wish to say to the future generations still yet to come? What stories, values, wisdom, and/or blessings do you wish to share? Just write what comes to you. This is where I leave you. For me, *Entrepreneurship Empowered* and this companion workbook are wonderful pieces of my beautiful legacy. I am building for 100 generations, if not more. I have done so by writing my truth and living in my authentic self. I am EMPOWERED. I thank you for being on this journey with me. I pray that you write the letter and receive yet another key. Again, the way out is within. Now go and live the EMPOWERED LIFE.

Personal Empowered Life Legacy Letter: _____

_____

_____

_____

_____

_____

_____

_____

_____

_____

EMPOWERED
LIFE™

Marketing Slogan Activity

Kid Tested. Mother Approved.
Life's Good
Trusted Everywhere
Maybe She's Born With It
We Try Harder
Keep Walking
Gather 'Round the Good Stuff
Makes Mouths Happy
Something Special in the Air
It's Not Just a Job, It's an Adventure!

Kix Cereal — The famous low sugar, round cereal!
LG Electronics — LG manufactures high quality flat panel televisions.
Duracell Batteries — Called "The Coppertop"
Maybelline — Maybelline was started in 1915!
Avis — Avis is headquartered in Parsippany, New Jersey.
Johnnie Walker — Johnnie Walker Scotch Whiskey is produced in Scotland.
Pizza Hut — Pizza Hut is owned by the same company that owns Taco Bell.
Twizzlers — Twizzlers flavors include chocolate, strawberry, and watermelon.
American Airlines — American Airlines is headquartered in Ft. Worth, Texas.
Navy — The Department of the Navy is a division of the Department of Defense.

Balance Sheet

Assets

Current Assets:

Cash	$12,000	
Accounts Receivable	$20,100	
Notes Receivable	$10,200	
Ending Inventory	$21,100	
Total Current Assets:		$63,400

Fixed Assets

Equipment and Vehicles	$111,000	
Buildings	$175,000	
Land	$250,000	
Total Fixed Assets:		$536,000

Other Fixed Assets

Goodwilll	$15,000	
Total Other Fixed Assets:		$15,000

Total Assets: $614,400

Liabilities and Owners Equity

Current Liabilities

Accounts Payable	$7,500	
Notes Payable (c)	$2,600	
Total Current Liabilities:		$10,100

Long-Term Liabilities

Notes Payable (L)	$35,000	
Bonds Payable	$10,000	
Total Long-Term Liabilities:		$45,000

Owner Equity

Common Stock	$316,000	
Retained Earnings	$243,300	
Total Owner Equity:		$559,300

Total Liabilities and Owner Equity: $614,400

Cost of Goods Sold

Calculate the Cost of Goods Sold if a business has:

     $14,000 cost of inventory at beginning of year

     $8,000 cost of additional inventory purchased during the year

     $10,000 ending inventory

Answer:

$12,000

You own a T-shirt business. At the beginning of the month, you have a T-shirt inventory balance of $300.00. During the month, you purchase an additional 100 T-shirts for $1,000.00. Then you sell some T-shirts. Thus, your inventory balance at the end of the month is $800.00. Calculate the cost of goods available for sale and the cost of goods sold for the month.

Answer:

$500

A company starts the month with $10,000.00 of inventory on hand, expends $25,000.00 on various inventory items during the month, and has $8,000.00 of inventory on hand at the end of the month. What is the cost of goods sold during the month?

Answer:

$27,000

Income Sheet
Revenue/Net Sales: $175,500

Cost of Goods Sold

  Beginning Inventory: $25,800

+ Merchandise Purchased: $52,800

Cost of Goods Available for Sale: $78,600

-   Ending Inventory: $21,100

Cost of Goods Sold: $57,500

Gross Profit: $118,000

Operating Expenses
  Salaries: $30,000
  Rent: $2,300
  Utilities: $1,400
  Advertising Expense: $15,000
  Insurance Expense: $9,000
  Interest Expense: $4,100
  Total Operating Expenses: $61,800

Net Income Before Taxes: $56,200

  -income taxes (33%): $18,546

Net Income After Taxes: $37,654

References and Resources

The following resources were used in writing this book and are duly noted in the text:

[1] Cherry, Kendra. (2019). "How Multitasking Affects Productivity and Brain Health." Verywell Mind. Accessed December 20, 2019.
https://www.verywellmind.com/multitasking-2795003.

[2] Neck, Heidi M., Neck, Christopher P., and Murray, Emma L. (2016.) *Entrepreneurship: The Practice and Mindset.* SAGE Publications.

[3] Daniel, C. (n.d.). "The 4 Animals Assessment." The 4 Animals Experience. Accessed December 20, 2019.
https://4animalsassessment.com/page-29740388.

[4] VARK Questionnaire. (n.d.). Accessed December 20, 2019.
http://vark-learn.com/the-vark-questionnaire/.

[5] Duckworth, A.L., Peterson, C., Matthews, M.D., and Kelly, D.R. (2007). Grit: Perseverance and Passion for Long-Term Goals. *Journal of Personality and Social Psychology.* Vol. 92. 1087–1101.
https://www.researchgate.net/publication/6290064_Grit_Perseverance_and_Passion_for_Long-Term_Goals.

[6] Microsoft Office 2010 Training Course — Revised 2018: Alison. (n.d.). Accessed December 20, 2019.
https://alison.com/course/microsoft-office-2010-revised-2018.

[7] USPTO Office of Public Affairs. (1994). United States Patent and Trademark Office. Accessed December 21, 2019.
https://www.uspto.gov/.

[8] Przybyla, D., Mehlmann, M., Rewari, and Dover, B. (2017). "The Psychology of Colors in Marketing and Branding." Accessed December 21, 2019.
https://www.colorpsychology.org/color-psychology-marketing/.

[9] Active Marketing website:
https://www.activemarketing.com/our-work/.

[10] Internal Revenue Service website:
www.irs.gov.

[11] Dun & Bradstreet website:
www.dnb.com.

[12] Small Business Administration (SBA) website:
https://www.sba.gov/.

About the Author

Ms. Palumbo is a business professional with more than 20 years of experience—17 as an entrepreneur. She is a creative leader with in-depth knowledge and expertise applying strategic business management, development of small business initiatives, and progressive leadership. Ms. Palumbo is an effective communicator with an innate ability to engage and hold the attention of those she trains and teaches. She owns several businesses, and she successfully grew her core business into multiple states. She is a social entrepreneur and has been serving the homeless community for more than 16 years. In addition to being an Empowered Entrepreneur, Ms. Palumbo is a Business Adjunct professor for several colleges in the greater Sacramento region.

Natasha M Palumbo, MBA
Author, Coach, Consultant and Speaker
Entrepreneur – Educator – Empowered

Instagram and LinkedIn: Natasha M Palumbo

natasha@entrepreneurshipempowered.com